Transitions
A Guide for the Transfer Student

Susan B. Weir

Oklahoma State University

THOMSON

WADSWORTH

Australia · Brazil · Canada · Mexico · Singapore · Spain · United Kingdom · United States

In memory of Dr. Marcia Dickman, 1949–2005

In honor of my husband, Tom,
with appreciation for his infinite
love and support

THOMSON

WADSWORTH

Transitions: A Guide for the Transfer Student
Susan B. Weir

Acquisitions Editor: *Annie Todd*
Editorial Assistant: *Dan DeBonis*
Marketing Manager: *Stacy Best*
Marketing Assistant: *Kathleen Remsberg*
Associate Content Project Manager: *Jessica Rasile*
Print Buyer: *Betsy Donaghey*
Senior Rights Acquisition Account Manager, Images:
Sheri Blaney

Photo Researcher: *Jill Engebretson*
Rights Acquisition Account Manager, Text:
Timothy Sisler
Production Service/Compositor: *Pre-PressPMG*
Senior Art Director: *Cate Rickard Barr*
Cover Designer: *Diana Coe*
Cover Image: © *Forrest Smyth/Alamy*
Cover/Text Printer: *Thomson West*

Printed in the United States of America
1 2 3 4 10 09 08 07

Library of Congress Catalog Card
Number: 2006940537

ISBN-13: 978-1-4130-2279-7
ISBN-10: 1-4130-2279-0

Thomson Higher Education
25 Thomson Place
Boston, MA 02210-1202
USA

For more information about our products, contact
us at:

Thomson Learning
Academic Resource Center
1-800-423-0563

For permission to use material from this text or
product, submit a request online at
http://www.thomsonrights.com

Any additional questions about permissions can
be submitted by e-mail to
thomsonrights@thomson.com

Photo Credits
P. 1 © David Butow/CORBIS SABA; P. 17 © John Giustina/Iconica/Getty Images; P. 35 © Design Pics
Inc./Alamy; P. 54 © Photolibrary.com Pty. Ltd./Index Open; P. 72 © BananaStock/SuperStock; P. 91 © AP
Photo/Journal & Courier, John Terhune; P. 109 © Susan Wides/Photonica/Getty Images; P. 127 © Seth
Joel/Taxi/Getty Images; P. 146 © ImageDJ/Index Open

Contents

Preface

Ollege student transfer from one institution of higher learning to another is widespread and is expected to continue. About 60 percent of students attend more than one institution at some point during their college careers, and community college transfer rates have increased about 10 percent over the past decade (Adelman, 2006). Transfer students are "first-year" students when they arrive at the receiving institution; however, they have experiences, needs, and expectations that are significantly different from those of native freshmen.

Although a planned and expected one-time transfer from one school to another can create uncertainty and risk in a college career, more complex attendance behaviors also contribute to concerns of students, faculty, and administrators. "Swirling" has become a common term to refer to a back-and-forth pattern of attendance between two or more institutions, particularly between two- and four-year schools (Adelman, 2006). Clearly, the traditional view of a college career encompassing four to five years at a single institution is a thing of the past.

Yet the unique needs and concerns of our growing population of transfer students have to date gone largely ignored. Orientation, first-year seminars, and other programming designed for freshmen falls precariously short in meeting the needs of these students.

Transfer students' prior experience in higher education can lead to "transfer shock"—a circumstance resulting from a sudden and often unexpected shift in policies and procedures, terminology, academic expectations, advising models, and culture from the previous institution to the current one (Grites, 2004). Native students as a whole are more successful at four-year institutions than are transfer students. These circumstances indicate clearly that prior college experience is often a poor predictor of future college success when institutional transition occurs.

Transfer students are an extremely diverse group in terms of age, college experience, ethnicity, academic goals, and academic expectations. Assessing and meeting the needs of this group is and will continue to be a challenge for educators.

This book was conceptualized and developed with the broad and diverse needs of transfer students, including nontraditional students, in mind. Many of these students have completed one to four semesters at a community college and are transitioning to a four-year regional or comprehensive university, and others have made the decision to move from a larger institution to a smaller one. Regardless of the nature of the shift, the changes in culture, terminology, expectations, and class size can make a seamless transition a daunting challenge for students.

This text is primarily designed for use in a junior-level first-semester orientation course for transfer students, but it could be easily used for sophomore- to senior-level students, or independently of formal classroom instruction. This text is appropriate for students regardless of whether or not they completed a first-year orientation course or seminar at a previous school. The content connects core academic success strategies with the exploration of critical higher-level cognitive skills and behaviors, particularly for those students who have stopped out for several terms before making the transition to their new institution. Areas of academic, personal, and professional concern unique to upper-class students, as well as nontraditional students, is emphasized.

For instructors who have not previously developed a transfer student orientation course, or for those looking to modify an existing course, this text can serve as the framework and guide. Each chapter contains a variety of elements that may be used in a classroom setting, or assigned for completion outside of the class. Questions for class discussion, activities designed to facilitate connection to campus, and journal assignments to encourage self-reflection are included in each chapter. This text is intentionally brief, thus allowing course instructors adequate time to incorporate institution-specific material during the course of the semester or term.

In conclusion, awareness of the academic, social, and psychological changes involved in college transfer would help facilitate and improve transfer student success (Lanaan, 2001). This text is committed to acknowledging and prioritizing the needs of a very large and important segment of today's college student population. As faculty and administrators work to meet the needs of transfer students, greater college success for a substantial portion of our student population can become a reality.

Acknowledgments

I would like to acknowledge the time and talents of many individuals who contributed to the conceptualization and development of this text. First, I would like to thank the Thomson Wadsworth team for their guidance, support, and expert assistance: Annie Todd, Daniel DeBonis, Carolyn Merrill, and Eden Kram.

Second, I owe my reviewers a note of genuine gratitude for the time and energy they have contributed toward this project. The expert insights, perspectives, suggestions, and validation that they have provided have proven to be invaluable as this text becomes a reality. The reviewers are:

Jeanie Allen, *Drury University*
Norm Barber, *University of Massachusetts, Dartmouth*
Mardi Craig, *Maryville College*
Russell Curley, *University of Cincinnati*
Sharon Gorman, *University of the Ozarks*
Cathy L. Hammond, *Morehead State University*
Scott Little, *Bellhaven College*
Terrie Minner, *University of Oregon*
Laynah Rogers, *Evangel University*
Nora Smith, *Montana State University*
Sandy Spann, *Greenville Technical College*
Kelli Stevens Webber, *Louisiana State University*
Steve Ward, *The University of South Dakota*
Ray Zarvell, *Bradley University*

Thank you all once more for your valued expertise and contributions to this book.

Plug In to Your New World!

1

> "Because transition is a process by which people unplug from an old world and plug into a new world, we can say that transition starts with an ending and finishes with a beginning."
> —William Bridges

In a Student's Voice

"I would tell new transfer students to come here with open arms, be able to accept people, and not get caught in someone else's negative pattern. Be open to learn new things. Be ready to experience something that you haven't experienced before, and just take it all in as it comes. Don't rush it."

—Chelsea, transfer student
(Nowak, 2004)

Learning Objectives

- Learn what to expect in the three phases of transition
- Understand the number and scope of college transfer students
- Become familiar with demographics of today's college population
- Become aware of your "locus of control" and reflect upon what this means to your college success
- Understand the role of self-motivation and goal setting in college success
- Understand the importance of feeling connected on campus

Quick Start Quiz

Assess your existing knowledge of key components of this chapter. Check each item below that applies to you:

❑   I know of at least three reasons why students transfer between colleges.
❑   I understand several major differences between traditional and nontraditional college students.
❑   I understand the importance of an internal locus of control.
❑   I am self-motivated.
❑   I am developing a strong sense of belonging at my new school.

Transition: What Does This Mean to You?

A transition is a person's experience with a major change in life. You've probably already experienced several transitions in your life—for example, moving from one home to another, beginning college, or perhaps getting married. Each change was likely a major turn of events as you began adapting to a new environment and developing new relationships. You may have had to give up some of your old habits and routines and learn new ones. It was certainly easy for your family and friends to observe that your life was entering a new phase when you made these changes. But what your family and friends may not have been able to perceive was how you felt about and dealt with that change—the emotional ups and downs, the challenges, and the social concerns that you had.

In his book *Managing Transitions: Making the Most of Change,* William Bridges (2003) describes the three phases of a transition:

- In the *ending phase,* you break away from an old way of doing things.
- In the *neutral zone,* you adapt to change. The old ways disappear, and you establish new beliefs, attitudes, and habits.
- In the *new beginning,* you possess a new identity—you set and achieve your goals in the new situation.

This model helps us to understand that the process of transitioning to a new environment takes time and effort. It isn't instantaneous or easy. The transition from high school to college was a significant one for you, and you probably learned many valuable lessons about what to expect in college, and learned how to adapt your lifestyle to the demands of college student life. However, the transition from one institution of higher learning to another can be equally challenging—and sometimes more so. You are adjusting to a new schedule of classes, a new campus, very likely a new city or town, and new terminology. You are perhaps juggling family and work responsibilities and managing an even tighter budget, all while facing a curriculum that may very well be more demanding than ever before. Let's apply William Bridges' model to your transition from one college to another:

1.   What is your *ending phase*? What kinds of behaviors or environments are ending for you? The answer to this question will be somewhat unique for each student. Consider your daily lifestyle. Are you moving from a commuter college to a residential college or vice versa? What is ending for you in terms of how you get to class? Are you changing from part-time student status to full-time or vice versa? What is ending regarding your daily routine? Next, consider academics. Are you enrolling in junior- and senior-level course work for the first time? What is ending regarding your study habits? What is ending regarding the content of your course work? Finally, consider your social network and leisure activities. Think about your friends, family, and the way in which you spend your free time; what endings can you identify?

2.   Consider what a *neutral zone* will mean to you. What new attitudes and habits will you be adopting during this transition? How long might it take to feel completely comfortable in your new environment? Think once more about your daily routine. Will you be starting a new part-time job? Learning new job duties and assimilating with a new group of co-workers always takes some time, and you may find yourself feeling frustrated as the "newbie" for a while. You may need some time to make new friends, meet your neighbors and new professors, and develop a real sense of belonging at your new school.

3.   Your *new identity* will evolve over time. You will eventually lose the notion of being a "new transfer" and will become a _____ Student (insert the name of your current school here). You will have a new daily routine, new friends, very possibly new study habits and a new job, new social opportunities, and new sense of purpose as your academic and professional goals materialize. Remember, the process of transition takes time. There will be some bumps along the road, but understanding what to expect will help you to navigate those bumps with skill, confidence, and optimism.

The purpose of this text is to help you learn what to expect as you begin your studies at a new school, and to give you some tools for overcoming any obstacle you may face in the coming weeks and months. This book is one tool to use as you progress from your ending to your new beginning. Remember, help is all around, but you must take responsibility for your own success—*it's up to you!*

Let's get started.

How Many Students Transfer Between Schools?

Thousands of college students transfer from one institution to another every year, and they comprise a substantial portion of the college student population. About one-third of all college students formally transfer at some point in their college careers (National Center for Education Statistics, 2004). About 60 percent of students attend more than one institution during college, even if they never formally transfer (Adelman, 2006).

Many students begin their studies at two-year schools (often also known as junior or community colleges), with the possible intent of completing a four-year degree after transfer. The U.S. Census Bureau reports that in October 2002, more than 16 million students were enrolled in U.S. colleges. Of those, almost five million, or about 29 percent, were taking courses at two-year schools. About one-half of the students who enroll in two-year institutions intending to complete four-year degrees transfer to four-year institutions within six years. About one-fourth of those who had initially only intended to complete two-year degrees change their minds and transfer to four-year schools or comprehensive universities.

Why do students transfer? There are many reasons. Let's begin with students who transfer from two-year to four-year schools; this is our largest group. If you're in this group, you may have always intended to complete a bachelor's degree, but decided to save tuition dollars by attending a community college for the first year or two. You may have also been able to live at home with your parents during this time, thus saving room and board costs as well.

Other students attend two-year institutions for the first year or two to build confidence in their academic skills, remain close to family and friends, explore academic and professional options, or complete mandatory general education course work even though they may already be admissible to four-year schools.

Although less common, transferring from a four-year school to a two-year school is not unusual. Many students find that the academic rigor or size of the four-year school is overwhelming during the first semester, or they may feel a little homesick. For them, completing freshman- and possibly sophomore-level course work at a school closer to home helps build the confidence, maturity, and study skills needed to return to the four-year school. And of course students do move from four-year to four-year schools, for an infinite number of reasons. Perhaps their preferred academic major was not available at the original institution, personal priorities changed, or a relocation was necessary due to family or military obligations.

So as you can see, students are moving from college to college for reasons that are as diverse as the students are! You are a member of an ever-growing group of college students who have made important personal decisions regarding the best way to complete their education.

Am I "Nontraditional?"

You may have heard the term "nontraditional" college student. So what does that mean, anyway? The "traditional" undergraduate student in years past has been defined as one who enrolls in college full-time immediately after finishing high school, is supported financially by his or her parents, and works few hours, if at all (National Center for Education Statistics, 2005). However, if we use this definition today, "traditional" students make up only 27 percent of the college student population. That would mean that almost three-quarters of college students are "nontraditional"! You may very well conclude that this definition is outdated. Women outnumber men on college campuses today, making up 56 percent of enrollment (National Center for Education Statistics, 2004), and you may meet students of every race on campus. Minority enrollments are rapidly growing. In 1976, only 15 percent of college students were ethnic minorities, but in 2002 that number reached 29 percent (National Center for Educational Statistics, 2004). As you walk across campus today, you may notice many differences in age, gender, and race. However, there are many differences that may not be visible, such as marital status, number of children, religious affiliation, or political views. Many students now choose to work full-time and attend classes part-time.

So who is "traditional" today? That's a tough question. Higher education has deep roots in tradition, but it changes continuously as our nation's people, needs, and social goals evolve. The purpose and nature of higher education has changed dramatically over the past 300 years or so, and the demographics of the students who attend college have changed as well.

The table on this page illustrates the proportion of U.S. residents who have completed high school; those who have earned college credits but have not completed a degree; and those who have completed a bachelor's degree or higher.

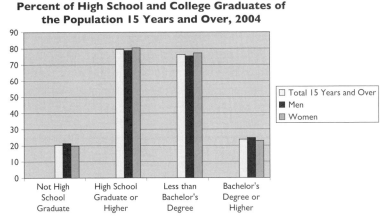

Percent of High School and College Graduates of the Population 15 Years and Over, 2004

Percentage of Total, Men and Women

Understanding the Liberal Arts

You may hear the term "liberal arts" from time to time in reference to many of the courses you are required to take in college. The term "liberal arts" dates back to the Middle Ages. "Liberal" comes from the Latin word "liber," or free. Liberal arts, then, were courses intended to educate free men, or the elite, as opposed to the "servile arts," which refers to trade skills needed by the workers employed by the elite.

Historically there have been seven liberal arts divided into two groups: the "trivium" includes grammar, rhetoric, and logic; and the "quadrivium" includes arithmetic, geometry, astronomy, and music. Trivium is Latin for "three roads," and it is a preparation for the quadrivium, or "the four roads."

As you work toward your college degree, you may wonder why you are being required to take courses that may seem irrelevant to your chosen major or professional path. Instruction in the liberal arts is necessary for students to develop general knowledge and intellectual skills, such as in language and reasoning, and stands in contrast to instruction for specific occupations, such as engineering, medicine, or business. Today, a university degree may consist exclusively of liberal arts courses, or it may combine a foundation in the liberal arts with courses in the major field that are more vocationally focused.

So I'm Here . . . Now What?

You are beginning an exciting chapter of your life. Your transition to your current institution may prompt all types of new challenges—social, academic, personal, financial, and emotional. Of all the community college students who transfer to four-year institutions with the intent of completing the bachelor's degree, only 39 percent are successful at completing that degree within six years (Berkner, He, and Cataldi, 2002). There are many reasons why students do not complete college; the better you understand those reasons the better prepared you'll be for the challenging road ahead. Let's identify some of these challenges so that you will have all of the tools you need to be successful in college and to graduate on time. Some first steps include taking control of your life, setting goals, and getting connected to your new campus.

Who's in the Driver's Seat?

If you took an introductory psychology class, you may have heard the term "locus of control." In a nutshell, this term refers to an individual's beliefs about the relationship of his or her behavior to his or her life events. A person with an "internal" locus of control generally believes that his or her behavior is a primary influence on life events. A person with an "external" locus of control generally believes that life events are the result of luck, fate, or the actions of other people.

Studies show that people with an internal locus of control ask more questions, have better problem-solving skills, and are more likely to achieve than those with an external locus of control. An internal locus generally leads to positive social adjustment and functioning as well as higher levels of self-motivation. These factors are critical to success in college, especially during times of stress and change. Keep in mind, however, that it is unrealistic to expect individuals to behave with either an internal or external locus of control all of the time—the idea is to try to lean toward thinking and behaving "internally" most of the time (Engler, 1999).

Activity

Do you have an internal or external locus of control? Take this short quiz to find out. For each item below, circle the response that most closely matches what you believe to be true.

1. A person who earns a lot of money in his or her job . . .
    a. Probably worked very hard to climb the career ladder
    b. Most likely got a lot of breaks from family or friends in the company

2. When I disagree with a policy at school or a law in my community, I . . .
    a. Make my views known to those in power
    b. Just accept it because "you can't fight city hall"

3. When preparing for an exam, I . . .
    a. Feel that the harder I study the better grade I can expect
    b. Feel that instructor grading policies are haphazard and unpredictable

4. If I fail the first assignment in a course, I . . .
    a. Speak with the instructor to find out how to improve next time
    b. Drop the course because there is probably little hope for improvement

5. When I disagree with someone, I . . .
    a. State my opinion in an effort to help them understand my position
    b. Change the subject because it is rarely possible to change someone's attitudes or beliefs

6. When I think about the coming school year, I . . .
    a. Know there will be challenges and feel ready to do my best to overcome them and succeed
    b. Know there will be challenges and hope they do not cause me to fail

As you probably have guessed, the "a" responses represent an internal locus of control and the "b" responses represent an external locus of control. Were most of your answers in one category or another?

If you would like to increase your level of "internal control," Santrock and Halonen (2006) suggest you try these strategies:

1. *Acknowledge your responsibility for outcomes.* Don't blame others for your failures. Be self-motivated.
2. *Go the extra mile.* When you put as much effort as possible into a task, you are more likely to feel you are responsible for your own success.
3. Say, *"I can do this!"* Positive attitudes toward challenging tasks will help you persevere and succeed.
4. *Get help when and where needed.* If you are not a strong writer, for example, find out where you can get assistance with your writing assignments. If you are a procrastinator, create a schedule and stick to it!

How Can I Accomplish All of My Goals?

A key factor in goal achievement is motivation. Motivation, simply put, is an incentive to do something. We are motivated at any given moment—perhaps right now you are motivated to finish reading this book chapter! We can feel motivated to lose weight, plan a weekend trip, adopt a pet, or complete a college degree. High levels of self-motivation can make the difference between a successful first year in your new environment, or a period of frustration and regret.

How do you motivate yourself? One important tool in self-motivation is *goal setting.* We all have goals. For example, if you're reading this book, chances are that one long-term goal you have is completing a bachelor's degree. You may also have future goals of landing a good job, earning a high salary, raising a happy family, and traveling. These are all reasonable goals to have. The problem is, they are not specific. When goals are not specific enough, it is hard to know how to achieve them or whether or not we've attained them. What is a "good" job to you? Is it a management position in a large corporation, or sole ownership of a small business? What is a "high" enough salary, in your opinion? You get the idea.

There is a big difference between a goal and a wish. The key to effective goal setting is to create long-term, mid-range, and short-term goals that are *specific, measurable, and realistic.* Goals must include not only the "what," but the "how"—what specific behaviors will result in achieving your goal?

Let's say your most important long-term goal right now is completing your bachelor's degree. That's a good start, but you'll need to be more specific. What specific degree will you complete—for example, do you intend to complete a bachelor of science or bachelor of arts degree? What is your major field? Will you graduate with honors? In what month and year will you graduate?

Next, create intermediate goals—specific, measurable, and realistic—that support this long-term goal. How many credit hours per term must you complete to graduate on time? Is this number realistic given your employment and/or family obligations? What grade point average do you need each term to graduate with honors?

Now, create even more specific, daily short-term goals to make sure you stay on track. Be sure to include how you will achieve them. For example, you might write down how many pages of reading you'll need to complete each day to keep up in each class. Better yet, write down exactly what pages in each book need to be completed. If a 15-page term paper is due at the end of the course, when is the best time to begin? If you create specific, manageable goals along the way, you can accomplish any large task without feeling overwhelmed. Let's use the term paper as an example. At mid-term, you might set a night to research your top three topics of interest and narrow it down to one topic. The next evening, plan to find five relevant sources on your topic and read them. The next day, make an appointment to visit with your professor about your research and develop a thesis statement. Specific, measurable, and realistic goals, established short-term, mid-range, and long-term, will help you stay on track, and as you observe your progress you will become more self-confident.

As you set your goals, there are strategies you can use to help you remain realistic and committed.

- *Determine the cost.* Commitment to a goal often means sacrificing time spent elsewhere. For example, spending more time studying at the library may mean fewer hours at work or with family. Consider what this new goal is costing you, and ask yourself if you are truly able to commit to the goal.
- *Write it down.* Putting your goal in writing will help the goal feel more real to you and others.
- *Just do it*! Get started today. Procrastination can quickly sabotage your goals.
- *A time of transition is a good time to begin.* You may feel that as you transition to a new life at your new school, and are making lifestyle changes on several levels, the time may be right to change your goal-setting habits.
- *Enlist support.* Talk to friends and family about your goals, and call on them for support when you feel discouraged or frustrated (Covey, 1998).

The Rewards for Completing Your College Degree

If you begin to feel extremely discouraged during your college career, and the thought of dropping out of school crosses your mind, consider your future earnings potential: the U.S. Census Bureau reports that workers 18 and older with a bachelor's degree earn an average of $51,206 a year, while those with a high school diploma earn an average of only $27,915. That's a big difference! Workers with an advanced degree (such as a master's or doctoral degree) earn an average of $74,602, and those without a high school diploma average just $18,734 (U.S. Census Bureau, 2005).

Activity

Practice setting goals. Read each item below, and rewrite each goal into one that is specific, realistic, and measurable, and includes not only the "what" but the "how." Here's an example: "I need to make more time for my family" is not a very specific or measurable goal. A better statement is, "From 7 to 8 p.m. every evening, my family and I will talk, play a game, or watch a movie together."

1. I will study more in History class.

    _____

2. I will lose weight.

    _____

3. I will save more money.

    _____

4. I will become a better writer.

    _____

5. I will do better in math.

    _____

6. I will get enough sleep.

    _____

How Do I Stay Motivated for the Long Haul?

Staying motivated each and every day is important, but it is not always easy to do. There may be times that despite the most careful planning, you're not able to accomplish the goals that you've set for the day. Don't give up! Setbacks are to be expected from time to time. When they happen, revise your goals to compensate for the setback. For example, due to an illness you may miss a few classes and feel ill prepared for an upcoming exam. Go the extra mile to make sure you get the information that you need. Make a plan to visit with your professor, obtain any handouts that you may have missed, and join a study group if you've not done so already.

If you find yourself setting goals that you continuously fail to achieve, you may want to contact a professor or advisor at your school to help you sort things out. It may be that the goals you are setting are not realistic for you, given your obligations outside of school. Or it could be that the course of study you've chosen is inconsistent with your aptitudes, values, or interests. It may be helpful to re-evaluate the choices you've made so far, and to investigate new options that you will be motivated to explore.

I Don't Quite Feel Like I Belong Here . . . What Can I Do?

Students who feel a strong sense of "connection" or "belonging" are more likely to complete college and enjoy their time on campus. Getting to know your advisor, your instructors, your classmates, roommates, and neighbors well is an important strategy for feeling connected and enlisting the support that you need.

There are many ways to connect to campus and develop healthy, productive relationships with others. The first level of connection will be your living arrangement. You may be sharing a room in a residence hall, sharing an apartment or house off campus with friends or family, living in a fraternity or sorority, or perhaps living alone. A happy and healthy living arrangement provides a solid foundation for college success.

If you are sharing living quarters with others, whether or not you have known your roommates for years or met for the first time just this semester, there are a few ground rules that can help you maintain a peaceful home.

- Have a discussion *now* about mutually agreeable rules before disagreements happen and feelings are hurt. Here are a few common areas of conflict that you will want to cover in your conversation:
  - Sleeping schedules. Do you and your roommates tend to retire at the same hour, or does one of you stay up later each night? If your sleeping schedules differ, decide now how late television or music can be on, and how loud. Also decide on lighting rules, if you share sleeping quarters.

○ <u>Personal property</u>. Some students feel that "what is mine is yours," when it comes to borrowing clothes, CDs, food, and so on, but others prefer to be asked permission before others borrow their stuff. Discuss your preferences now, before that pink sweater you had saved for Friday night is missing!

○ <u>Visitors</u>. We all enjoy entertaining from time to time, but how much is too much? While many students enjoy company, others prefer privacy. Create some ground rules now regarding how often you'll be having visitors, and how long they stay.

○ <u>Study time</u>. If you plan to do part or all of your studying at home, create a schedule now to share with your roommate(s). They will need to know when you prefer not to be disturbed and when to keep the noise level at a minimum.

- When disagreement or conflict does occur, pick your battles carefully. If you are sharing living space for at least a year, you'll need to work on preserving your relationships. Think before you speak.

- Always treat your roommate(s) with respect. Regardless of your feelings, it is important to treat them and their property as you wish you and your property to be treated. When things are not going well, this simple rule will help all of you live together as peacefully as possible.

The second level of connection to campus is in your classes. Get to know your classmates and your professors. In smaller classes, participate in class discussion as much as possible. Introduce yourself to others and learn their names. If you are a shy person, it may feel awkward at first, but with practice you'll feel more confident initiating conversation. You may find that you have multiple classes with some of the same students. In larger classes, if you tend to sit in the same area each day, introduce yourself to those seated near you.

On Your Campus

This week, arrive a few minutes early to each of your classes, and introduce yourself to two or three people you don't know. You may find that this is an easy way to make new friends and possibly study partners.

Depending upon the size and mission of your new school, your professors may have different responsibilities than at your previous institution. Large universities have several different missions: usually teaching, research, and service (also called extension or outreach). Your professors may be engaged in all three of these activities. They may teach just one or two courses each semester, and spend the rest of their workday in a university research lab, in departmental meetings, or supervising student groups. In contrast, faculty members at small or medium-sized regional colleges may focus primarily on teaching, and teach several more courses each term than their counterparts at large universities. Research may not be a major expectation.

Faculty Titles

You may see many different titles accompanying your professors' names. It can be more than a little confusing. Although rankings and policies vary from university to university, here is a general idea of how the academic titles are typically assigned in higher education:

- Lecturer or adjunct faculty: An individual who is hired to teach a specific course or combination of courses on a temporary basis. Generally this position is not eligible for tenure. (Tenure is a status granted when the faculty member has satisfied certain performance criteria established by the academic unit, and tenure generally provides long-term job security. Tenure allows faculty to enjoy academic freedom in teaching and research.)

- Assistant professor: This title is generally assigned to new permanent faculty members. Assistant professors will generally hold the terminal (or highest available) degree in their field. They are generally eligible for tenure and must meet certain performance criteria in a limited time to be promoted, tenured, and continue to be employed at the university.

- Associate professor: An assistant professor is promoted to associate professor when he or she has completed a specified number of years at the university and has performed at a designated level in a combination of teaching, research, and service (criteria vary between academic programs and institutions). Generally tenure is awarded at this point.

- Professor (also known as full professor): An associate professor can be promoted to professor after a further period of meritorious service specified by the university.

- Professor emeritus: These faculty members are generally retired, but may teach or conduct research on a limited basis.

You may find that some of your instructors are not professors, but are graduate students. These are master's or doctoral students who are teaching classes or lab or discussion sections in exchange for a stipend and/or sometimes all or part of their tuition. They are usually called teaching assistants, or TAs for short. If you have a TA, it does not necessarily mean you are receiving an inferior educational experience. TAs and professors vary widely in their levels of teaching experience, enthusiasm, organization, presentation skills, and charisma. Students vary widely in their learning styles and individual interests. Regardless of the rank of your instructor, it is in your best interest to get to know him or her and to make the most of your experience in class.

A third level of connection to campus is with your academic advisor. Many colleges require students to meet with an advisor at least once each term, before registering for courses. Your advisor may be a faculty member in your academic major, or your advisor may be a professional staff member who is specifically trained in advising. Whether or not advising is mandatory at your school, you should make the effort to get to know your advisor well. He or she plays a fundamental role in helping you to learn all of the requirements for your degree, helping you plan for a timely graduation, helping you find campus resources (such as career planning, counseling services, volunteer center, and so on), and can generally help direct you to the proper offices for the myriad of questions you will have as a new student on campus. We'll talk more about the role of advisors in the next chapter.

A fourth level of connection to campus happens in student organizations. While school, work, and family obligations can account for nearly all of your time each week, if possible, make time to participate in at least one student group or club. Participation in such groups not only helps you meet people and make friends, but can provide you with leadership experience, community service, planning/coordinating skills, and many other types of experiences that employers seek. Think of this as time taken to build a strong and well-rounded resume.

Finally, take time to have fun on campus and enjoy your school spirit! Find out what is going on via your school newspaper, flyers on campus, or talking with classmates. Try to actively participate in one or two activities or events each semester that will be fun for you.

? Questions for Class Discussion

1. Consider the term "nontraditional student." What does that mean? Who is "nontraditional" on your campus?
2. Higher education today serves the dual purpose of creating well-rounded, educated citizens as well as preparing students for professional careers. Which outcome is most important to you? Why?
3. What challenges have you faced so far as a transfer student? What challenge has been the most stressful for you? How are you coping with this challenge?
4. Is it easy or difficult to set and achieve goals? What are some of the challenges you face in this process?
5. What do you do to stay motivated? What helps you get back on your feet after a setback?
6. What student organizations do you know of on campus? Have you decided to join? Why or why not?

Journal Assignment

In your journal this week, reflect on the locus of control exercise. Write one to two pages. To direct your writing, please consider and answer these questions:

1. Do you believe you have a predominantly internal or external locus of control?
2. What life experiences do you believe contributed to your perspective?
3. How will your locus of control impact your experience in college?
4. What changes to your perspective, if any, would you like to achieve? How will you achieve this?

Summary

- As a transfer student, you're not alone! About one-third of students formally transfer to a different school at some point in their college careers.
- There are many reasons to begin at one institution and transfer to another, including financial, personal, academic, and social considerations.
- The "traditional" college student of yesteryear is no more! Today's students are more ethnically diverse than ever; many students work, some full-time; many are married with children; and enrollment of women slightly outnumbers that of men.
- Your "locus of control" may be a factor in your college success. Determine what perspective you have, and reflect on how that may impact the coming year.
- Goal setting is one important way to find the motivation you need to be successful in college.
- Feeling connected to campus can help you persist in college.

Case Study

Derek had big plans for college, and had hoped to attend Delta State University right after high school—after all, his father and older brother were both alums. Not only that, three of Derek's best friends were also planning to attend DSU; all four hoped to rent a house together off campus.

Sadly, however, Derek did not score high enough on his college entrance exams to be admitted to DSU as a freshman. His three friends did get accepted, and they enrolled at DSU with the hope that Derek would be able to join them the following academic year. So Derek enrolled in the local community college, and he completed one year of course work while living at home with his parents. At the end of the year, Derek had completed the minimum requirements to be admissible to DSU as a transfer student. He was thrilled and confident that he had the skills to be successful at his new school. Derek moved in with his three friends to the rental house the following August.

Life at DSU was fantastic. Derek enjoyed a vibrant social life and several buddies he could call on for help with anything. Derek had not yet decided on a major, but he did not worry too much about that, as he had another semester or two before he finished all of his "basics." Derek did know he wanted to complete his college degree, because he did want a good job, but he had not given much thought to specifics. Derek's father was a bit nervous about Derek's lack of focus, and had warned him that he would not finance Derek's education past the first four years. But again, to Derek, all that was far into the future.

Derek generally attended classes, but he did find himself skipping from time to time when something else seemed more appealing, such as an impromptu volleyball game on the front lawn of the house or a much-needed nap after a late night of partying. After all, Derek reasoned, he needed exercise, and plus, if he was tired he would not be able to pay attention in class anyway. Derek did not worry too much about earning high grades during his first year at DSU, as he felt that his classes were just the basic, boring liberal arts classes that he was required to take and did not seem to offer much value in his future. He would be sure to work much harder when he got into the classes for his major field of study.

Derek's father and brother warned him about making time to study, but Derek thought, hey, if I just want to scrape by with a C average, then what's the fuss about? And yes, Derek felt that he did take time to get caught up with reading and studying—usually pulling an all-nighter before exam day.

At the close of the semester Derek was shocked to discover that he had earned a 1.5 grade point average. He would be suspended from DSU if he did not bring his grades up to at least a 2.0 in the spring. Derek was embarrassed and anxious, and he was not completely sure why his first semester had resulted in disaster.

Food for Thought

What assumptions did Derek make that ultimately undermined his grades? What can he do differently now with his motivation and goal setting?

Building a Foundation for Success

2

> "Life loves to be taken by the lapel and told, 'I am with you, kid. Let's go!'"
>
> —Maya Angelou

In a Student's Voice

"I found out pretty quickly that at the university I needed to present myself to other people. I used to be quite shy, and people kind of took that as snobbery. And I found through experience, it just pays more to really, you know, go out of your way, and meet that other person. Because, especially in a university this big, the more friends you have, the better off you are. When I went to community college I would get up there, go to my classes, and go home. I really didn't make an effort to make friends up there because I had friends in my hometown I would see each night. Here I've kind of come out of my shell. I've gone out of my way to meet new people. I don't think I really have changed anything about my behavior, but I feel like I have a more worldly perspective by being part of this campus because it's so diverse."

—Ann, transfer student
(Nowak, 2004)

Learning Objectives

- Understand the reasons for transfer shock
- Become aware of the curricular, emotional, financial, and academic issues that can sabotage success
- Learn strategies to overcome challenges in each area
- Understand the role of academic advising on campus and the student's responsibility in the advising process
- Understand the role of technology in your education

Quick Start Quiz

Assess your existing knowledge of some key components of this chapter. Check each item below that applies to you:

❑   I understand the reasons why many transfer students experience "transfer shock."
❑   I know what behaviors my professors expect of me.
❑   I know what types of behaviors my academic advisor expects of me.
❑   I understand my rights as legislated by FERPA.
❑   I feel comfortable using the technology that my new school expects me to use.

What Is *Transfer Shock?*

If you're an experienced and successful college student, then you should be ready for success at any other college . . . right? Research in higher education over the years indicates that more than likely the transition will not be as smooth as you had hoped it would be. Transfer students come to their new campuses with a broad range of experiences, attitudes, and competencies. In this chapter we'll discuss some of the challenges that transfer students typically face, and we will explore some tips for ensuring your success.

Transfer shock is a term that refers to the set of experiences you may have during your first semester or two at your new institution that may lead to unwanted circumstances. For example, many students experience homesickness or feelings of isolation. Some students feel overwhelmed academically and begin to lose self-confidence and self-esteem. Most students experience a drop in grade point average. In severe cases, some students may drop out of college altogether. But don't panic just yet. Students can avoid or bounce back quickly from transfer shock if they are aware of what it is, can identify their particular vulnerabilities, and take the appropriate steps to reduce or eliminate problems.

Lynch (1994) identified several factors contributing to transfer shock. Transfer shock results from unexpected outcomes in a variety of areas, including the following:

1. <u>Curricular concerns</u>. Generally most of your previous course work will "transfer" to your new school. This is what many students are told as they enroll each semester at the previous institution. This statement is technically true, but it can be very misleading. The whole truth is while most courses will "transfer," *some courses may not apply to your chosen degree program.* For example, you may have chosen a biology course to fulfill a science requirement at your first school, only to discover that your intended degree requires physics instead, and the biology course was not needed at all. Or you may have taken several classes in your intended academic major, only to find that your new school does not accept any transfer work in the major requirements. These situations may leave you feeling frustrated because you

feel you've wasted time and money, or because you realize you will need more time than you expected to complete your degree.

What to Do?

- First of all, realize that education is intrinsically beneficial—just because it won't "count" toward your major does not mean it is wasted or worthless.
- Second, meet with your academic advisor and create a long-term plan that will help you graduate as closely as possible within your intended timeline (more on that later).
- Finally, contact your financial aid office for information if you feel that you may run short on funding for an additional unforeseen semester or two.

2. <u>Emotional concerns</u>. Attending a school close to family and friends is a good way to maintain the necessary emotional support during the transition from high school to college. But what happens when you leave that comfort zone? Anxiety is common when students move away from family and friends, especially if it is for the first time. The transition from one college to another can be just as difficult as the initial adjustment from high school to college. Just when you need it most, suddenly there are no familiar faces in the classroom, or at home when you return at the end of the day. Your self-confidence and self-esteem may begin to suffer.

What to Do?

Create a new network of support—in other words, make new friends! Seek out all of the support that you can. And do it soon. Here are some tips:

- Join a campus organization or club. Most schools have a wide variety of clubs that cater to just about any interest you may have: academic, athletic, spiritual, cultural, or special interest clubs that may support a cause such as the environment or community service. In addition to making new friends, you'll be building your resume.
- Get to class a few minutes early and strike up a conversation with your neighbor. Don't be shy—your neighbor may be a transfer student with many of the same questions and concerns that you have.
- Live on campus if you can. Often, transfer students are sophomores or juniors who feel that the residence halls are only for freshmen—not so! By living off campus, students miss out on opportunities to meet other students easily, get involved in residential governance, or join study groups. Also, studies show that students who live on campus generally have higher grade point averages than students who live off campus! Even if you're married and/or have children, ask about campus housing—you may be surprised at what your school has to offer for you.

- If you've tried some of these strategies and still feel disconnected or even depressed, contact your university counseling service. Many universities provide confidential professional counseling either free or at reduced rates to students.

3. Many students have <u>financial concerns</u>. Indeed, for many students, financial matters are often the primary roadblock to degree completion. Transfer students often have even more financial responsibilities, especially those transferring from a two-year to a four-year school, or from a public to a private school—tuition is generally more expensive. It is very common for transfer or nontraditional students to pay their own way through school, and many of these students are supporting one or more family members as well. For these students, working part- or even full-time is a necessity. How can you ensure you'll have enough money for college? Creating and sticking to a budget, keeping track of expenses, actively seeking scholarship and grant opportunities, and avoiding credit card debt are important. We'll go into more detail on these matters in Chapter 7.

4. <u>Academic concerns</u>. The academic culture and climate are usually very different between one school and another, particularly when transferring between schools of differing sizes and missions—for example, from a community college to a comprehensive university, or from a large public institution to a smaller, private one. Some institutions are primarily focused on teaching, while others include research and extension. Most faculty at comprehensive universities are required to conduct ongoing research in addition to teaching classes. These obligations may contribute to limited availability to students outside of class. If you are returning to college after a semester or more out of school, you may need a little extra support. Check out the "Returning Student Strategies" on the next page for a few tips.

What to Do?

- Make an extra effort to get to know your instructors early. Faculty will generally be available to meet with you during scheduled office hours, or by appointment. It is useful to visit individually with your professors—before you need help—so that they know you are a committed and serious student. Then, if and when you do need extra assistance, you will already have established a positive working relationship, and discussing your difficulties may be a bit easier for you. Not sure what to talk about? Bring up a topic that you found interesting in class, and perhaps ask where to find more information on the subject. Ask about your professor's areas of research. If you enjoy the class, let your professor know! You could even ask what other courses in the discipline he or she would recommend. Finally, in the event

ON-TARGET TIPS

Returning Student Strategies

■ *Evaluate your support system.* A strong and varied support system can help you adapt to college. If you have a partner or family, their encouragement and understanding can help a lot. Your friends can also lend support.

■ *Make new friends.* As you seek out friends of different ages, focus on meeting other older students. You'll find that many other older students also juggle responsibilities and are anxious about their classes.

■ *Get involved in campus life.* The campus is not just for younger students. Check out the organizations and groups at your college. Join one or more that interest you.

■ *Don't be afraid to ask for help.* Learn about the services your college offers. Health and counseling services can help you with the special concerns of older students. These include parenting and child care, divorce, and time management. If you have any doubts about your academic skills, get some help from the study skill professionals on your campus.

that you do not need any extra assistance throughout the term, and you do well in the class, the relationship that you've established will make it easier to ask for a letter of recommendation for upcoming scholarship, employment, or internship opportunities.

On Your Campus

This week, explore student clubs and organizations. Find three that may be of interest to you, and make an appointment to interview the club president or faculty advisor. Ask about the purpose and mission of the organization, scheduled activities, and requirements or benefits of membership. And if you're interested, sign up!

How to Get Along with Your Professors

If you want to establish a productive, positive relationship with your professors, you will need to behave in a respectful and professional manner in the classroom. Specifically, this means:

> Arrive on time or early to class
> Turn off your cell phone ahead of time
> Sit near the front
> Wear clean clothes that are in good repair
> Sit up straight in your chair

continued

> Give the professor your full attention
> Stay for the full class period
>
> Conversely, avoid the following behaviors:
>
> Acting bored or sleeping in class
> Talking while the professor is lecturing
> Reading the newspaper during class
> Wearing headphones
> Eating or chewing gum loudly
> Asking "Did we do anything important?" after missing class
> Complaining about the difficulty of the course
>
> If you adhere to this advice, your relationship with your professors will be off to a healthy and productive beginning.

- Identify responsible students in your classes and get to know them. These will be the students who attend every class meeting, arrive on time or early, sit near the front, pay attention, and ask questions. These are the students you want to get to know and perhaps even form a study group with.

Defining "Adulthood" in College

The term "in loco parentis" is Latin for "in the place of the parent." This term described the relationship of faculty with their students in the early days of higher education, in the 17th and 18th centuries. Students were often rebellious and rambunctious, and faculty developed strict rules of discipline, sometimes threatening suspension or expulsion for any type of disobedience. Fortunately for students, this "parent–child" perspective declined over time, and by the 20th century, students began to be regarded more or less as adults, albeit not in a legal sense. Then, in 1971, the Twenty-Sixth Amendment lowered the voting age to eighteen, thus legally defining the concept of adulthood. Today, college students are viewed socially and legally as adults—even if they enroll before age 18—and are expected to be responsible and accountable for their behavior.

How Can My Advisor Help?

You may have visited with an academic advisor (or academic counselor as it is called at some schools) at your previous institution. So chances are you are familiar with the role of the advisor. But now, more than ever, you should acquaint yourself with the services that your advisor can provide, as well as your responsibilities as an advisee.

Academic advising may be mandatory at your new school, or it may be optional. Either way, your tuition dollars are paying for this service, and it is highly recommended that you participate fully in the advising process.

Your advisor may be a faculty member in an academic department, or your advisor may be a professional staff member in a student services office. Both advising models have their own advantages and disadvantages. Faculty advisors are experts in their fields, and can offer you in-depth information concerning their disciplines. However, due to their other responsibilities, their office hours may be limited. Professional staff advisors are often experts in college student development, and may be trained in a more generalist fashion concerning degree programs and career paths. It is common for staff advisors to be available to see students during the majority of a normal workweek. But either way, your advisor is there to help you learn how to be a successful college student. Some students view advisors as people who simply assist them with class registration each semester. A good advisor does much, much more than that.

Get to know your advisor *well.* Advisors do what they do because they enjoy working one-on-one with students. Your advisor will welcome your interest in becoming fully engaged in the advising process. Here are some of the things that your advisor can do for you:

- Help you learn and understand all of the requirements for your degree. Remember, ultimately it is the student's responsibility to ensure that all graduation requirements are met. Your advisor is there to *help you learn and understand,* not to foster your dependence on his or her knowledge. Don't be afraid to ask lots and lots of questions.

- Help you develop a long-term plan of study. If you want to graduate in a timely manner and avoid unpleasant surprises, sit down with your advisor and create a semester-by-semester plan that includes every course requirement. This is especially helpful if you're incorporating a minor or second major, or requirements for admission to graduate or professional school, or even teacher certification. The more academic goals you have, the greater the need for careful and detailed planning. Furthermore, the courses you need may not be available every semester. So get an expert's advice and assistance. See Appendix A for an example of a long-term plan for a student with multiple academic goals.

- Help you find the assistance you need in any area. For example, are you worried about taking a math course? Your advisor may be able to recommend a tutor or math resource center. Are you concerned about job prospects in your chosen field? Your advisor can often tell you where recent graduates in your major are now working. Are you looking for scholarships? Again, your advisor can direct you to the proper campus office. If you have a question or problem and don't know where to turn, it usually is wise to start with your advising office.

- Help you understand university policies and procedures. For example, if your grades aren't turning out to be what you expected first semester, or if you need to withdraw from a course or two, your advisor can explain academic retention standards and options for you.

Here are a few things advisors will *not* do for you (although students sometimes expect them to):

- Make decisions for you. Your advisor is not your parent. Your advisor is here to help you gather the information that you need to make adult, autonomous, informed decisions about your education and your future.
- Guarantee your success. Your advisor can offer an immense amount of guidance and information, but the bottom line is that students are responsible for their own success or failure. Ask questions, and when appropriate, request information in writing.
- Bend the rules. Advisors must be consistent and fair, often with large numbers of students. Academic standards must be upheld for both legal and ethical reasons. It is good to get to know your advisor well, but don't expect special treatment regarding policies.

In return, your advisor will expect students to:

- Contact your advisor whenever questions or concerns begin to arise. Don't wait until a problem has turned into a crisis!
- If your advisor prefers to see students by appointment, make and keep your appointments, and arrive on time. Don't expect your advisor to be available for you at the drop of a hat. Most advisors have additional responsibilities that take them out of the office, and high numbers of advisees may keep their calendars booked.
- Prepare for your advising meetings by making a list of your questions, and/or a tentative list of courses (if you're visiting about enrollment).
- Consider talking to your parents about your grades. Federal law (see "Family Educational Right to Privacy Act (FERPA), 1974" on the next page) prohibits advisors from sharing your academic information with outside parties without your written permission. Parents sometimes call advisors for information about their children only to be informed that such information cannot be released to them.
- Keep your address, telephone, and e-mail information current with your advisor and with university records so that you can be reached when necessary.

Family Educational Right to Privacy Act (FERPA), 1974

FERPA is a federal law that protects the privacy of student educational records. FERPA allows parents the rights to access their children's records before the child enters college. These rights transfer to the student when he or she turns 18 or enrolls in college. So now that you are in college, your parents or others outside the institution may not access your educational records without your written permission. If you are a dependent, and your parents supply your school with the most recent copy of their tax return documenting your dependency, then the school can release your records to your parents.

FERPA does allow disclosure of your records to other school officials with a legitimate educational interest—for example, your professor could discuss your performance in class with your advisor. And of course your records can be released to authorities when required by law (for example, if issued a subpoena). Schools may disclose, without consent, "directory" information such as a student's name, address, telephone number, date and place of birth, honors and awards, and dates of attendance. If you do not wish such directory information to ever be disclosed outside of the university, you can request your records to be flagged so that university officials will know of your preference. Contact your admissions office or registrar for the procedure.

While FERPA helps to protect your privacy, it also prevents your family from knowing how you are doing unless you tell them. Think about your family's role in your education, particularly regarding emotional support. You may want to keep your family informed so that they can be an active part of your support network.

Activity

Take this quiz and find out what areas may become a concern for you. Jot down "yes" or "no" next to each question.

1. Did the majority of your family and/or your friends support your decision to transfer colleges?
2. Are you moving away from home for the first time?
3. Are you financially responsible for yourself?
4. Are you a single parent?
5. Are you returning to college after taking a break for one or more semesters?
6. Do you feel confident in your academic preparedness?
7. Do you work more than 20 hours per week?
8. Do you have an academic major in mind?
9. Do you commute more than 20 miles to campus?
10. Do you have friends or family locally?

These questions represent some of the challenges transfer students around the country face as they make the transition to the new school. Score your quiz this way:

1. Yes = 2 points;   No = 1 point   My score _____
2. Yes = 1 point;   No = 2 points   My score _____
3. Yes = 1 point;   No = 2 points   My score _____
4. Yes = 1 point;   No = 2 points   My score _____
5. Yes = 1 point;   No = 2 points   My score _____
6. Yes = 2 points;   No = 1 point   My score _____
7. Yes = 1 point;   No = 2 points   My score _____
8. Yes = 2 points;   No = 1 point   My score _____
9. Yes = 1 point;   No = 2 points   My score _____
10. Yes = 2 points;   No = 1 point   My score _____
                                      Total: _____

Your score will be anywhere between 10 and 20, with lower scores suggesting a greater risk of problems ahead and higher scores suggesting a relatively lower risk. If your score is closer to 10 than 20, don't panic—you will be successful in college with some careful planning and extra effort in certain areas. Let's address each area in turn.

1. Did your family and/or your friends support your decision to transfer colleges? If your answer is no, you may lack some of the emotional support you need when stress is on the rise. Seek support from those around you, such as neighbors, roommates, classmates, professors, and new friends. Don't be shy about reaching out for assistance and reassurance.

2. If you're on your own for the first time, you may find yourself responsible for tasks that may be new to you . . . meal planning, shopping, paying the bills. Take stock of what will change for you and plan accordingly. For example, if you're planning your own meals for the first time and don't particularly enjoy it, you may be tempted to rely on fast food. In this case you may find yourself gaining weight, lacking energy, and spending more money on food than you intended (more on this in Chapter 9). Your college experience may mean learning new skills in the kitchen!

3. Being accountable for all of your income and expenses is ultimately a positive goal in life; however, for students it can be a source of frustration and anxiety. Students frequently live month to month with little to spare. Despite the best budgeting and advance planning, inevitably something unexpected leaves you short on cash—an unexpected automobile repair; a medical expense not covered by insurance; a last-minute airline ticket. If you have a family member who can bail you out in an emergency, so much the better, but if not, try your best to keep a savings account active (more in Chapter 7)!

4. Are you a single parent? More so than most students, you'll need to take advantage of campus and community resources. Make sure you have a responsible friend or two in each class who can take notes for you, should a child's illness keep you at home for the day. Keep the lines of communication with your advisor and your professors open. Keep them informed—in advance, when possible—of any circumstances that require you to miss class.

5. Are you returning to college after taking a break for one or more semesters? Taking a break is not necessarily negative—many students need to *stop out* in order to earn tuition money or to take stock of their academic goals. But sometimes a break can leave you academically rusty. You may need to refresh your skills in some areas.

6. Many students feel insecure with their levels of academic skills, particularly in mathematics, science, and writing. If this applies to you, ask your advisor where you can get supplemental instruction or tutoring.

7. Do you work more than 20 hours per week? College is expensive, and it's no surprise that many students work more than they like, given their course loads. Time management is critical. You will become a master at multitasking and efficiency (more in Chapter 6).

8. Have you declared a major? While major and career exploration are expected during the freshman year, it is often difficult to progress much farther academically as an undecided student. Why? For starters, many majors include course sequences that begin early. You may fall behind if you wait too long. Secondly, many students find it difficult to remain motivated in college if they are not sure what their academic and professional goals are. If you need help with this decision, visit your advisor or career services office soon.

9. Do you commute more than 20 miles to campus? If so, you already know the investment you're making in terms of time, gasoline, vehicle maintenance, and even missed classes when the car won't start or the weather is foul. Investigate your alternatives carefully. If moving closer to campus is not an option, look into carpooling.

10. Do you have friends or family locally? When crises occur it helps to have trusted friends to whom you can turn for assistance. If not, get to know your neighbors and classmates.

Technology: Friend or Foe?

Students arrive on campus with vastly different experiences and attitudes about technology. Some carry a laptop and a PDA (personal digital assistant) wherever they go; others have never owned a computer and have yet to use e-mail. If you fall into the first category, you will probably adapt well to the use of technology on campus. If you fall into the second category, hold on and get ready to learn some new skills!

Most colleges expect students to use computers. The level of use may vary from expecting students simply to check university e-mail accounts to requiring all students to own a laptop. You will almost certainly use the Internet from time to time for research; you may even take an entire course online. Many colleges provide a Web-based student information portal where students can access their academic records, update their contact information, and even register for classes. It will be a good idea to make sure your level of skill and comfort with technology matches the expectations of your college.

Your first mission on this journey will be to make sure you have access to a computer. If you have your own computer, you'll need to be sure that you have Internet access at home. Check with your information technology department for details on both on- and off-campus access. If you have wireless Internet access capability, find out where the campus "hot spots" are.

If you do not own a computer, explore the locations and hours of the campus computer labs. Stop by frequently throughout the first few weeks to determine when the busy times are—you'll definitely need to plan ahead when it comes time to type your term papers. Assume that the computer labs will become busier as the semester progresses. Pre-finals week may be a mob scene!

You may find purchasing a computer to be a worthwhile investment—it can be frustrating to print out a term paper in the lab, then come home and pull it out, only to see a glaring typo on the first page. Back to the lab you go!

If you choose to purchase a computer, you will have to do some research in order to select the right machine for your needs and your budget. Here are some important considerations:

- Laptop or desktop? A laptop is helpful if you type your class notes and want to keep them handy as you study or do research away from home. It is also a space saver in a small apartment or residence hall room. The downside? Laptops are huge targets for thieves on campus. You will have to be extremely vigilant when you carry your laptop with you. Laptops are also generally more expensive to purchase than desktops. Some newer desktops include flat screens and compact CPUs that are much smaller than their predecessors. Consider your lifestyle, budget, and available space to determine which model is better for you.
- What about hardware? Now we're getting really technical! Here are some key terms that you will want to understand as you research your computing options:
  - Operating system: Software that allows you to run computer applications.

○ Central processing unit (CPU): Main compartment that houses the processor that carries out the operating system's commands. Processor speed influences the speed of your machine.

○ Random Access Memory (RAM): The more RAM you have, the more applications you can be using at once, and the faster your computer will run.

○ Macintosh: A model of computer manufactured by Apple Computer, Inc. The Mac's operating system is usually preferred for graphics, music, and video applications. You can expect to find the Macintosh used in art, graphic design, journalism, and music departments.

○ PC: Personal computer. The term PC is generally used for a wide range of brands of machines that use Windows as the operating system. The majority of machines used in higher education are windows-based (Ellis, 2006).

• Your school may offer a student discount with certain manufacturers for both hardware and software. Find out and compare the school discount with the best price you can find on your own.

How Can I Use the Internet Effectively?

"The Web has become the 'new normal' in the American way of life; those who don't go online constitute an ever-shrinking minority." (Pew Internet and American Life Project, 2005).

The advent of the Internet in the late 20th century has dramatically changed the way we work and the way we learn. Assignments that once required a trip to the library searching for books and articles can now often be completed in the comfort of your home. The problem is, the Internet is not as organized as the library. It is not trustworthy, either—Web sites can be outdated or contain intentional misinformation. Just about anyone can post a Web site about anything at all. You can find Web sites developed by young children! Searching effectively for quality sources takes some skill and practice.

If you are working on a research paper, you will probably need to use scholarly journals as your sources. Your university library may offer electronic access to databases of scholarly journals, allowing you to search for articles specifically related to your topic. Some articles are available as full-text documents that you can print. Some are not and will require a trip to the library to find the article and make a photocopy. You will find more detail on this process of research in Chapter 5.

If you are seeking general information on a topic and do not have a specific source in mind, then you may need to conduct a wide search for your topic using an Internet search engine. There are many search engines from which to choose. You might want to experiment with them to find the one that best suits your needs. Search engines use a computer program to find Web pages that contain the search words you specify. To help narrow your search, use Boolean operators: AND, OR, and NOT. If you are looking for an exact phrase, enclose the phrase in quotation marks. Some popular search engines to try:

- www.google.com
- www.search.yahoo.com
- www.dogpile.com
- www.altavista.com
- www.hotbot.com

See which search engines come up with the most relevant results for your project.

As you explore your search results, you will need to critically examine each Web site before using the information that you find. Not all sites are trustworthy or accurate. The first step is to *consider the source*. The Uniform Resource Locator, or URL for short, is the Web site's address and will offer some basic information about the nature of the organization that has developed the Web site. A URL ending in *.edu* usually represents a school, college, or university; *.org* represents a nonprofit organization; *.gov* represents a government agency; and *.com* represents a for-profit commercial enterprise. However, there is a lot of crossover in Internet extensions, and you cannot always rely on them for accuracy. Ask yourself these questions: Is the person or organization that developed the site clearly indicated? Is the Web site professionally designed and free of grammar and spelling errors? Is there a mailing address and telephone number listed?

Next, consider the *quality of the information*. Is the information based on fact or opinion? Are sources of information cited? Is it current? Many sites include a feature indicating the date (and often time) the Web page was last updated.

Finally, as you choose your sources of information, always cite appropriately in your paper. Never copy or paraphrase Web sites without attributing the information to the proper source (more on this subject in Chapter 5).

Internet Use in America

On a typical day in 2004, *70 million Americans* went online to check e-mail, read the news, book travel reservations, get medical or health information, gamble, participate in auctions, shop, seek out romance, and participate in countless other activities. This represents a 37 percent increase from the year 2000 (Pew Internet and American Life Project, 2005).

What About Technology in the Classroom?

Many faculty members use electronic tools such as Blackboard, WebCT, or Desire2Learn as part of a traditional class. These Web-based course management programs enable students to access presentations, readings, tests, and assignments; they also allow students to view their scores as assignments and exams are graded. Students and faculty can also participate in threaded discussion or chat sessions.

These tools are also used for courses that are taught exclusively online or as part of a "hybrid" format (i.e., 80 percent online and 20 percent in class).

If you will be responsible for using this technology, be sure to log in and become familiar with the setup and requirements as soon as your class begins. You will want to feel comfortable using this technology as due dates and exam dates approach. You may also want to set up a contingency plan in the event of a crisis. For example:

- Make sure you have current contact information (office location and telephone and fax numbers) for your professor in case you lose Internet access.
- If you normally use your home computer, identify a campus computer lab that you can use and its hours of operation, in case your computer crashes or you lose Internet access.
- Locate your campus computing help desk so you can get assistance if you have technical difficulties that you cannot resolve.

Oh Yeah . . . What About My E-mail?

Electronic mail (e-mail) can be a useful tool for communicating with your professors, advisor, and classmates. If you already use e-mail, you probably know there is no shortage of mail each day when you log in to your account. Reading and sending e-mail messages has become a standard and time-consuming part of our workday.

Sadly, with the growth of e-mail communication, we also see the growth of "spam," or unsolicited junk mail. Often you can identify spam by an unfamiliar e-mail address and a suspicious or vague subject line. However, spammers often create programs that will forward spam from your e-mail account to others in your address book, thus creating the appearance of an e-mail from a trusted friend or colleague.

Whether you've used e-mail for years or are just now getting started, there are some important guidelines to follow that will help you use e-mail productively and help you minimize the effects of spam.

- <u>Use your university e-mail account</u> if one is provided to you. Your professor or advisor may expect you to check it daily. Also, if they need to send a message to you, your university e-mail address is one they can access. Additionally, your professor may create a class listserv using only university accounts.

- <u>Be specific in your subject line</u>. A specific subject line helps your recipients to know what your message is about; how urgent it is; and may help them know that the message is valid. For example, if you are writing to your professor, a subject line such as "Need Help" is not as useful as this: "Lisa Cole's question about Physics 101." Including a familiar name in the subject line helps the reader verify that the message is one they should open and read.

- <u>Use proper grammar, spelling, and organization</u>. It is tempting to view e-mail as very informal communication, and resort to a "stream of consciousness" style of writing without regard to mechanics. This can be frustrating to your readers—it will take more time and energy to clarify your question and may take a follow-up e-mail to fully understand your inquiry. Also, proper use of language sends a message of respect and professionalism to your readers, which is always a good idea when communicating with your professors.

- <u>DON'T USE ALL CAPS</u>. It seems as though I'm screaming at you, doesn't it? In most day-to-day correspondence, use of all caps is considered rude and inappropriate. If your message is urgent, flag your message appropriately using your e-mail system delivery options.

- <u>Consider your timeline</u>. Don't use e-mail in emergencies. If you have a question about an assignment due an hour from now, pick up the telephone and call your professor. There are no guarantees that faculty check messages every hour or even every day. Here is a guideline: if you need assistance or information in less than five days, pick up the telephone or visit in person.

- <u>Manage your e-mail inbox</u>. Create a schedule for checking and responding to messages on a regular basis. If you expect your readers to open your e-mail correspondence in a timely fashion, extend the same courtesy to them when they write to you. Delete messages regularly to free up space and make sure your e-mail account does not become deactivated. If you need to save messages, create folders and organize them accordingly.

- <u>Protect your privacy</u>. E-mail is not private. Be careful what you write. One way to minimize your level of risk is to assume your messages will be forwarded to the president of the university or to *The New York Times*. Do not include your social security number or any other vulnerable information in e-mail messages. If you need to discuss confidential matters with your professors or advisors, do so in person. Do not send e-mail when you are angry or emotional—you may regret it later. E-mail evidence can be recovered and used in a court of law.

If you have read this far and are feeling very uncomfortable with the idea of integrating computer use into academic life, talk to your advisor about the possibility of taking a beginning computer applications course. The skills you learn in such a course will transfer to many of your future courses, and they will help to build your comfort level and self-confidence!

? Questions for Class Discussion

1. What did you anticipate would be your greatest challenges as you prepared to transfer to this school?
2. Were your predictions correct? What unanticipated challenges have you faced?
3. What are the expectations for the use of technology on campus? Are they similar to those of your previous school? How are they different?
4. What should be the role of the parent in a college student's education?
5. How has e-mail and instant messaging changed the way you interact with your friends and family? Is this good or bad?
6. What kinds of things are you doing for the first time in your life now? Is this change positive or negative for you?

Journal Assignment

Based on the activity earlier in the chapter, what challenges do you expect to face this year? Write one to two pages. To direct your writing, consider answering these questions:

1. What challenges do I face this year?
2. Which are the most stressful for me to think about?
3. Where can I turn for help?
4. What are three things I can do now to cope with these issues and maximize my college success?

Summary

- Transfer students arrive on their new campuses with high hopes and great expectations of success. However, the transition is not always a seamless one.
- "Transfer shock" refers to the various challenges transfer students face that can result in a grade point average decline during the first semester or two.
- Students may have curricular, academic, financial, and emotional concerns.
- Take stock of your challenges and create a plan for success.

- Getting to know your academic advisor, creating a long-term academic plan, and using assistance on campus can help.
- Understand the technology expectations at your school and become familiar with using computers, the Internet, and e-mail.

Case Study

In high school, Ashleigh was unsure of what her academic major would be in college. She and her family decided it would make sense to attend the state's large comprehensive university, Metro U, and explore a number of career directions. Ashleigh did well her freshman year, had a healthy social life, and took advantage of several opportunities to investigate major and career options.

After speaking to her zoology professor, and doing some research in her campus career resource center, Ashleigh decided she would like to earn a degree in marine biology. Unfortunately, being far away from the ocean, Metro did not offer such a degree program. After reviewing her options, Ashleigh transferred to Seaside College, a smaller private institution about a day's drive away.

Ashleigh felt ready to live off campus after a year in the residence halls at Metro. She did not know anyone at Seaside, so she rented an off-campus apartment by herself. She figured that she would go home once a month or so to see her old friends, and although she hoped to make some new friends at Seaside, she did not go out of her way to do so.

Lacking the meal plan provided in the residence halls, Ashleigh found herself needing to shop for groceries and cook for herself in her new apartment. This did not appeal to Ashleigh very much—after all, she was spending a lot of time studying, was rarely at home at mealtime, and just did not like to shop or cook. So she tended to use the drive through lane at fast food outlets on her way to and from campus each day. She knew that the nutritional value of these meals was not terrific, but it did save time, so this arrangement solved the problem for the time being.

After the first semester, however, Ashleigh found she had gained 15 pounds, was tired all the time, and due to eating out almost daily she had run out of the money that she hoped would last the entire academic year. She did not have the money for gas to go home as often as she wished. On top of that, she had not made any friends at Seaside. She felt alone and frustrated with herself.

Food for Thought

What decisions did Ashleigh make that led to her situation? What can she do now to change things?

Study Skills I

3

"It is not enough to have a good mind; the main thing is to use it well."

—Rene Descartes

In a Student's Voice

"At community college the class sizes were like 20, 50 at most. The professors actually knew if I was there and after a week or so they got to know my name. I got a lot of individual attention. They also could tell if I had a problem that might be affecting my work. We did more work in the classroom; here it is like all I am doing is taking notes. I do most of my work at home, alone. It's a good thing I started at community college where they could explain the basics and I could actually feel comfortable asking questions in class. I am a good student, but I would have felt intimidated in the size of the classes here."

—Alan, transfer student
(Nowak, 2004)

Learning Objectives

- Become aware of the level of academic expectations at your new institution
- Understand the time commitment involved in full-time study
- Learn basic strategies for success— the 3RM method
- Understand the importance of regular attendance and good lecture notes
- Become aware of the potential challenges in mathematics
- Learn strategies for test taking and relieving test anxiety
- Understand the rules of academic integrity
- Become familiar with campus resources that may assist you

Quick Start Quiz

Assess your existing knowledge of key components of this chapter. Check each item below that applies to you:

❑ I know how much time I should commit to outside study for every hour spent in class.

❑ I can describe at least one strategy for retaining information I read in textbooks.

❑ I have a specific plan for using my study time effectively.

❑ I know where to turn for help on my campus, should I need assistance with course work.

❑ I can name at least three behaviors that are considered violations of academic integrity on my campus.

What Is Changing for Me in the Classroom?

You may find that you need to spend more time on schoolwork than ever before. The academic expectations at your new school will be different, and they may be more challenging. If you are transferring after your sophomore year, then you will probably be taking primarily upper-division course work, and upper-division work is usually much more demanding. You will likely find that the volume of material that you'll be responsible for has increased, as has the depth of understanding required.

But you do not have to have earned a perfect ACT or SAT score to be successful at your new school. Academic success is related to many factors, such as motivation, self-discipline, and resilience when setbacks occur, as well as continued dedication and commitment to your goals. In this chapter, you'll learn some basic strategies that you can use to meet the academic challenges ahead.

➡ STRATEGY NUMBER 1 ▪ Academics Come First

If you are transferring from a two-year school to a four-year school, or from a smaller institution to a larger one, you may find that there are many, many more social opportunities, extracurricular programs, campus events, and other social or personal outlets that may be of interest to you. While it is important to make friends, get involved, and feel that you belong at your new school, it is also vitally important to establish your personal boundaries. Setting priorities will be critical. Chapter 6 will discuss more on this topic. To succeed academically, you'll need to make school your *first priority*. After all, if you're a full-time student, you have a full-time job!

Consider this guideline: in general, to earn good grades, you'll need to spend about two to three hours outside of class for every one hour spent in class. If you're enrolled in 14 credit hours, that translates to 14 hours spent in class per week, plus at least 28 hours spent reading, studying, doing homework, and writing papers, for a minimum of 42 hours per week devoted to school. The amount of time you spend on each class may vary depending on your aptitude for the subject and your professor's expectations.

You should plan on allocating the proper amount of study time each week from the very start of the academic term. Even if homework and reading seem light at first, by staying current with the syllabus you can minimize the headaches and stress that can occur when the larger and time-consuming midterm assignments and exams come up.

☑ **Tip:** If you have other obligations, such as employment, children, or volunteer work, talk with your boss or your family now about the time that you need to devote to your schoolwork. Make adjustments now that you can live with to be sure that you have allocated the proper amount of time for school and that no aspect of your life goes unattended. Employers and family members who understand your academic obligations can and should become part of your support network. If you have children at home, you might consider establishing a "family study time" each evening. This way you can attend to your studies and your children will, too. There will be more on time management in Chapter 6.

Your Course Syllabus

A course syllabus is a document prepared by the course instructor. It will usually be distributed on the first day of class, or you may be directed to a Web site where you can download it to your computer or print it out.

Make it a practice to *read every word* of your syllabus on the first day of class and make sure you understand it. Why? The syllabus is essentially your contract with the professor of the course. The syllabus will help you learn what is expected of you and help you allocate the proper amount of time studying for the course and completing assignments. Additionally, the information regarding content and any prerequisite course work will help you confirm whether or not you wish to remain enrolled in the course. If after reading the course syllabus you are not sure whether or not the course is appropriate for you, discuss the matter *immediately* with your instructor or with your advisor.

If at any point in the semester you feel that an assignment has been graded inconsistently with the criteria stated in the syllabus, contact your professor for clarification or correction.

➡ STRATEGY NUMBER 2 ▪ Active Learning

Have you ever read a chapter in a textbook, closed the book, and were unable to remember much of what you just read? Many students make the mistake of believing that simply reading over the material a time or two will be sufficient for retaining the information and ensuring success on exams. However, this strategy does not commit the material to long-term memory and will prepare you to answer only the most basic of exam questions, at best. An *active* learner becomes much more *engaged* in the process of reading and learning.

So how does one become "engaged"? Nist and Holschuh (2002) describe one strategy, called the "3RM" method: Reflect, Rehearse, Review, and Monitor.

Reflecting means thinking about what you have just read. Put it in your own words. Make sure it makes sense to you. Think of examples and jot them down. Explain it to a friend. By doing so, you'll ensure that you really understand what you are trying to learn. Here's an example. Let's say you are taking a psychology course, and you are learning about the theories of Sigmund Freud. Your textbook, *Personality Theories*, contains the following paragraph:

> "Adult dreams also express unsatisfied wishes, but, because in the adult many of these wishes have become unacceptable to the self-concept, the dream is in disguise. Therefore, Freud distinguishes between the manifest dream and the latent dream. The manifest dream is the dream that is remembered the next morning. Such a dream frequently appears incoherent and nonsensical, the fantasy of a mad person. Nevertheless, it presents some kind of narrative story (Gloria, 1991). The latent dream refers to the meaning or motive underlying the manifest dream. Analysis seeks to discover the latent meaning that is expressed within the manifest dream. The dream wish, however, has undergone distortion, and its mask must be removed before it will reveal its meaning" (Engler, 1999, p. 37).

"OK," you might say to yourself . . . "how can I explain this? In adults, according to Freud, dreams are about unsatisfied wishes. Freud believes these wishes may be unacceptable to us, and therefore he views dreams in two ways. The manifest dream is the actual story or sequence of events—no matter how silly—that you remember when you wake up. The latent dream is the real meaning of the dream that the manifest dream covers up. If I were undergoing psychoanalysis, my therapist would try to determine the latent meaning of my dreams."

Then, you should try to think of an example . . . perhaps a dream that you had recently and what you think the latent meaning might be. Jot down those examples in your text next to the appropriate paragraph—when you can relate a concept to your own experiences, chances are you'll remember it much more easily!

Rehearsing means repeating the information so that you can remember it. You should rehearse both verbally and in written form. One effective way to do this is by creating concept cards. A concept card is a note card with a detailed definition of a term on one side, and the name of the term on the other. In order to organize your concept cards, you should include the larger concept and the page in your text where it is discussed on the side with the term. It might look something like this:

Freud's theory of psychoanalysis   Engler p. 37

Manifest vs Latent Dream

If you make and keep concept cards for each course in your book bag, you can pull them out whenever you have a free minute and rehearse, rehearse, rehearse. It's a convenient way to study that does not require sitting at a desk with text and notebook at hand.

Reviewing is something like rehearsing but takes it to the next level. The purpose of reviewing is to make sure you understand your concepts, relate them to other main concepts in the course, and ensure that what you have learned so far becomes firmly rooted in your long-term memory. If your instructor provides a study guide before exams, this will be most helpful in guiding the review process. If not, you can create one for yourself. List the main concepts that you'll be tested on, and ask yourself detailed questions. Use words like "how" and "why" rather than "what" in your questions in order to make sure you're reviewing in depth. In the example we've been using, you might ask yourself, "How does Freud distinguish between two different types of dreams?" It is also useful to create a study group for the review process—you can ask each other these questions, and have help explaining difficult concepts to each other.

Monitoring means keeping up with the pace of the class and making sure you understand everything as you go along. If you don't understand what the instructor is explaining in class, by all means ask him or her to repeat the information, or to explain it a different way. You might also visit your instructor during office hours if you realize after class has ended that you're confused about a topic. The key idea is to keep up with your reading and assignments, and to act promptly if you are not comfortable with or do not understand the material. If you wait until just before an exam to clarify the material, you may find there is quite a lot you did not thoroughly understand, or you may not have time to seek out the information you need. In addition, this realization can leave you feeling overwhelmed and can erode your confidence during the exam.

The Easiest Way to Avoid an F

Tragically, sometimes students earn a failing grade in a class and don't even realize it! How can this happen?

Your new school will have deadlines for adding and dropping courses each semester. They may be very different from your old institution, and transfer students must learn the new policies. Timelines and penalties for adding and dropping can vary significantly from one school to the next. You should find drop and add deadlines in your course syllabus, or if not, your advisor or registrar's office can provide this information for you.

Sometimes students intend to drop out of a course in which they have enrolled, but they simply forget to do so until after the deadline to drop has passed. Or they may believe they have completed the proper drop procedure, only to find out at the end of the term that they did not. Many schools use a Web-based course registration system, and students may find it takes a little practice to use this correctly.

If you do not correctly drop a course and miss the deadline, you are in danger of earning a failing grade for the course. It may not be possible to retroactively remove the failing grade; institutional policies will vary.

Bottom line: Be sure to learn what your school's drop deadlines and procedures are. If you need to drop a course, follow the procedures in a timely manner, and be sure to obtain a printed copy of your new class schedule as verification that the drop has been processed.

On Your Campus

This week, identify the one or two courses this semester that will be the most difficult or time-consuming for you. Then research campus resources that will help—for example, tutoring services, writing centers, or math and science resource centers. Take action now to have any necessary support or assistance ready when you need it.

➡ STRATEGY NUMBER 3 ▪ Take Good Lecture Notes

Most of the time the material covered in lecture will appear on your exams. And much of the time the material covered in lecture is not covered in your assigned reading! So you'll need to take good notes.

The most important first step in taking good notes is regular class attendance. Some students adopt the notion that class attendance is optional, and once in a while a professor will explicitly tell you that attendance will not be mandatory—but you will still be responsible for the material covered in class. It is critical for you to be in class and to take good notes. Don't rely on a friend to take notes for you—many students take lousy notes! Here are a few pointers for effective note taking.

1. Sit near the front. This helps to ensure you can see and hear clearly, and also makes it easier to ask questions. You are less likely to be distracted by the activities or conversations of other students.

2. Concentrate on the lecture. All of us have differing attention spans, so do what you need to do to ensure that your mind does not drift away. If you sit in front (item #1) that helps! You should also make sure you're not overly tired or hungry. If your neighbor insists on chatting (less likely if you sit in front!), kindly ask him or her to wait until after class.

3. Don't take down every word. There will typically not be enough time to take notes in narrative form—at least not legibly! Write down key terms, use abbreviations, arrows, and circles to connect ideas.

4. Listen for clues. Your professor will typically emphasize key points that you need to learn well. Draw attention to these points in your notes with circles, underscores, or asterisks.

5. Ask questions. If you don't understand something, raise your hand and ask. Chances are, if you are confused, others in your class may be as well. If you make sure you understand what your professor is explaining as he or she goes along, you're doing a good job of monitoring, too!

6. Review your notes after your lecture and before the next lecture. Fill in any details you remember but did not have time to jot down. Some students prefer to type their notes after class as a way to further organize and review the material. When you return to class, ask your professor for clarification of anything you did not understand from the previous class meeting.

Some Common Abbreviations to Use in Lecture Notes

b/c = because
e.g. = for example
w/ = with
w/o = without
< = less than
> = more than
~ = approximately
@ = at
** = this is important!
??? = I don't understand; seek clarification from instructor

➡ STRATEGY NUMBER 4 ▪ Conquering Mathematics

Is the thought of a math class about as appealing as a root canal? If so, you're not alone; many students find mathematics to be especially challenging. If you are a returning student and are taking math after a long hiatus from high school or college-level math, what you learned in the past may be long forgotten. But chances are you're going to have to do what it takes to complete at least one or two college-level math courses. Here are some tips to help you:

1. Do not procrastinate! Math skills are like muscles: use 'em or lose 'em. The longer you wait, the more you will forget from the last time you completed a math course; then you'll find yourself needing to review your previous course work in order to make sure your skills are at the proper level for your next course.

2. Make sure you understand how much math you will need for your chosen major. Math requirements vary by degree program. If you're math phobic, you may not be happy in a major that requires calculus or above. Have a heart-to-heart with your advisor or a career counselor if your interests and goals don't appear to be a good fit with your aptitude for or interest in mathematics.

3. Take a placement test. Many institutions will require or at least offer a placement test in math. The last math course you took—although similar in name—may not have included the same content as a similarly named course at your new school. So you may or may not be ready for the next level. A placement test is an objective way to find out exactly where your skill level is now.

4. If you need remedial math, *take it*. Some students are tempted to skip remedial math and enroll in college-level math against better advice. Remedial courses cannot count for college credit; therefore, some students see them as a waste of tuition dollars. However, skipping a recommended math course is a huge risk. If placement test scores indicate that you need a remedial math course, think of the course as an investment in your future success. A failing grade in college-level math will do much more damage to your wallet and to your transcript than money spent on the proper course for your present skill level.

5. Engage in positive self-talk. Build your self-confidence by telling yourself, "I am capable and can become an 'A' student in math." Imagine the boost of pride and encouragement you will feel as you work hard to see this statement materialize.

Once you've enrolled in the appropriate math course, here are some ways to ensure your success:

1. Find a tutor at the beginning of the semester. Don't wait until you do poorly on the first assignment or quiz. It helps to be sure you thoroughly understand all of the material as you go along, and furthermore, there may not be any more tutors available on campus if you wait until mid-term to find one.

2. Enroll with a friend or make a new friend in class. Choose a student who is as responsible and committed as you are. You will have an automatic study partner and built-in emotional support!

3. Make math your priority. Don't miss class, take good notes, ask questions, and most importantly, keep up. Do more than just the minimum homework problems. Place your math homework first on your study agenda each day. Practice, practice, practice!

4. As you solve problems, ask yourself: does my solution make sense? Many silly mistakes can be avoided with this simple double-check system (Nist and Holschuh, 2002).

5. Get to know your math instructor. Make appointments or visit during posted office hours when you have questions about the material covered in class. Let your instructor know of your commitment to earning high grades in class.

American College Trends

Between 1700 and 1900, somewhere between 1 and 5 percent of Americans between the ages of 18 and 22 enrolled in college. After World War I this figure increased to about 20 percent. By 1960 about 33 percent of this age group enrolled in college, and by the 1970s the number rose to almost 50 percent. Today, around 70 percent of Americans have some college credit, although only 25 percent or so actually have completed bachelor's degrees.

➡ STRATEGY NUMBER 5 · Study Smart

Your approach to study time will impact your academic success dramatically. Unlike scheduled class meetings, or the hours you are required to be at work, study time is not mandated to occur at a specific time and place and therefore is easy to forget about if you do not have a specific plan in place. Here are a few "Dos" and "Don'ts" as you develop your personal study plan:

- DO allocate study time into your schedule *every day*. This allows you to review lecture notes when they are fresh in your mind. If there are any issues from your most recent class meeting or most recent assigned reading that you do not fully understand, you can make a list of questions to ask your instructor before the next class meeting. Daily study time helps commit material to long-term memory—a must for optimal learning and minimal stress on exam day.

- DO minimize distractions during your allocated study time. Let your family or friends know when you will be studying and that you are not available during this time. Set your cell phone to "silent" or "off." Make sure you are not overly hungry, tired, or anxious. If you're worried about something in particular, make a note to focus on the issue when your study session is complete.

- DO study on campus. Generally speaking, this is a better idea than studying at home. Your campus library is likely to be a good place to find quiet nooks with desks and chairs and minimal distractions. Plus, you'll have quick access to books, articles, or Internet resources, should you need them. If you have an hour break between classes, spending this time in your favorite library study nook is a wise use of your time.

- DO make sure you have everything with you before you leave for your designated study area. Returning home for forgotten texts, notes, calculators, or other materials will drastically reduce your productive study time.

- DO study your most difficult subject first. This will help ensure that you allocate an adequate amount of time to the material, and that your energy level is high. Attempting to understand complex material when you are tired or feeling rushed is usually not productive.

- DO take breaks from time to time. Monitor your attention span to determine how often you may need a break. A 5- to 10-minute break every hour or every 90 minutes usually works well. Fresh air, a brisk walk around the building, a stretch, and a light snack will help revive your energy and attention to your task.

- DON'T allocate study time when your energy level is at its lowest. Some of us are "morning people," and some of us tend to be more alert later in the day or evening. Try to allocate your study time when you are reasonably awake and alert.

- DON'T pull all-nighters before an exam. "Cramming" is not effective learning. The night before an exam is your time to reinforce the material that you have already learned, not the time to be reading the material for the first time. Students who pull all-nighters are prone to more stress, more fatigue, and minimal learning. As the sun begins to rise, these students may even decide to nap for "just a few minutes," only to awaken hours later and discover—in horror—that they have missed the exam altogether.

- DON'T study with friends who are more interested in socializing than studying. It will be annoying and time consuming for you to continually attempt to keep everyone on task. If you do study in groups, decide on a few ground rules in advance—create scheduled breaks for chatting, eating, and so on.
- DON'T study in bed. You may find that study time quickly turns into nap time! To maintain your attention, find a reasonably comfortable chair, and sit up straight while you study.
- DON'T be tempted to exchange your daily study time for another activity with plans to make up the time later in the week. We humans are creatures of habit. If you abandon your commitment to a daily study habit, new habits will form, and before you know it, study time has become erratic at best. Self-discipline is critical for maintaining your level of commitment to academics.

Procrastination

Are you a procrastinator? Do you tend to put off for tomorrow the things you know you should do today? A lot of people do, but it doesn't help you to be a successful college student, nor does it help you to be successful in your many other life roles. Procrastinators tend to perform poorly on tasks that they could otherwise do well, given adequate preparation and attention. It is tempting to use procrastination as an excuse for rushed or sloppy work.

How can you avoid the pitfalls of procrastination? Create a schedule and stick to it (more details in Chapter 6). Don't give yourself the option of postponing a task. When more appealing options arise, such as a phone call or social invitation, let friends or family know you will join them at a later time or date. Kicking the procrastination habit, and accomplishing your goals, will help your self-confidence to blossom!

➡ STRATEGY NUMBER 6 · Effective Test Taking

Exams are a requisite piece of college life. Yet many students dread exams and find them a constant source of anxiety and worry. But hey, let's get crazy for a minute . . . could exams possibly be fun? Believe it or not, yes, they can. If you arrive to the exam well prepared, rested, and self-confident, you will enjoy the opportunity to demonstrate to your professor all that you have learned.

The first step to achieving the proper level of preparedness is to follow the study skills and strategies outlined earlier in this chapter. Go to class, study every day; study effectively (use the 3RM method); ask questions; obtain assistance when needed. Make sure you know what topics will be covered on the exam and how many points (or what percentage of your final grade) the exam is worth. What types of questions will be on the exam? How many items will be on the exam and how much time will you have? If your course syllabus does not specify, ask your instructor for clarification. Knowing what to expect can help boost your confidence and peace of mind on exam day.

When you are handed your test, scan the entire document to determine exactly how many items are included. Look for easier questions and answer those first. Keep track of the time and work efficiently, but do not rush.

It is useful to familiarize yourself with strategies for approaching each type of exam question. Here are some tips:

Multiple Choice

- Read the stem slowly and carefully. Reading quickly sometimes causes students to miss critical words such as NOT, OR, NEVER, or ALWAYS.
- Cover up the response choices with your hand and try to answer the question in your head.
- Then, lift your hand and consider each response choice. Sometimes more than one choice could reasonably be considered correct; your instructor may be looking for the *best* choice.
- If you are somewhat unsure of the best choice, begin by eliminating response choices that are clearly incorrect. Then consider the remaining choices carefully.

True/False

- As in multiple choice, you must read true/false statements extremely carefully. Missing one critical word can cause a reversal of the meaning of the statement. Look for qualifiers such as NEVER, ALWAYS, SOME-TIMES, or RARELY.
- Carefully consider each number, fact, date, or assertion in a true/false question. A slight deviation in fact can signal a false statement.
- Check your work. If you've identified a statement as being false, ask yourself what modifications would make the statement true.

Essay Questions

Essay questions require good analytical, organizational, and writing skills, and they can be vexing for many students. Yet essay questions are an opportunity to demonstrate the depth of your learning—a well-prepared and confident student will welcome essay items. Here are some strategies to help you become an expert essayist:

- Note the number of essay questions on the exam and budget your time accordingly. If you have insufficient time to write all that you know, it is better to write a few sentences for each question than to leave a question blank.
- Before you begin to write, jot down a brief outline in the margin of your paper. An outline will help prompt you to include key terms or ideas, and to keep your essay organized.
- Always write as legibly as possible and use just one side of the paper for maximum readability.
- Use proper grammar, spelling, and punctuation.
- Underline key terms as you write so they are sure not to escape your professor's attention as he or she reviews your essay.
- Support each main idea with examples and with as much detail as you know.

Test Anxiety

Many students suffer from what is known as "test anxiety." Although a little bit of anxiety is productive—it helps keep us alert and focused on the task—a high degree of anxiety is counterproductive. You may be experiencing a high degree of test anxiety if you notice sweaty hands, a racing heartbeat, nausea, and a general feeling of dread as you enter the classroom on exam day. If these symptoms sound familiar, there are some steps you can take to ease the problem.

- Make sure you are prepared for the exam. If you diligently follow the advice in this chapter, chances are you will notice your anxiety level diminish considerably.
- Visualize yourself completing the exam confidently. Imagine you are at your chair with the exam on your desk. Imagine the pride and confidence you feel as you answer one question after another quickly and correctly.
- Stop negative thoughts. Often students with test anxiety get into a pattern of creating excuses such as, "I just don't test well," or "I am not as smart as the others in this class," or "this professor is just too hard." Replace this type of thinking with positive self-talk. For example, "I have studied hard and am ready to ace this exam," or "I am just as smart and capable as anyone else in the room." A positive attitude is critical!
- Get a good night's sleep before the exam. It is a good idea to review your notes the night before, but not at the expense of sleep.

- Don't go into the exam hungry. Eat light, nutritious foods an hour or more before the exam so that you maintain your energy level and do not become sleepy. Use caffeine in moderation if at all—caffeine can increase anxiety.
- Conduct deep breathing exercises to help you relax before going into the exam room. Find a quiet space. Stand or sit with your eyes closed. Inhale as deeply as you can. Let the air out slowly. Free your mind of any thought or worries as you do this. Repeat several times.

These strategies can help you on exam day and in other situations that you find are stress-inducing. It may take a few attempts to feel comfortable with this new routine, so practice often!

➡ STRATEGY NUMBER 7 ▪ Know Where to Turn for Help

Despite your very best efforts, you may find that you are not doing as well in class as you had expected. Most college campuses have many resources designed to help you succeed in just about any area you need. Don't be shy about asking for assistance—after all, your tuition and fee dollars are funding these resources! Here are a few examples of the types of services you may wish to explore:

- *Tutoring Services:* Many campuses have an office that will connect you with another undergraduate student who has a well-established record of success in a particular discipline, or a tutor may be a graduate student in the field. Some services are free, and some tutors charge an hourly fee.
- *Supplemental Instruction or Review Sessions:* Some academic units coordinate regular sessions to provide additional coverage of the material from lecture, or group sessions to help you review material and ask questions before an exam.
- *Academic Success Seminars:* You may find group sessions that will help you learn general success strategies, such as effective note taking and textbook reading; preparation for final exams; or how to reduce your anxiety before an exam.
- *Counseling Services:* Adjustment to a new college environment is seldom easy. Students must deal with all kinds of issues, including homesickness, loneliness, anxiety about school, family problems, or feeling overwhelmed. When this happens it becomes extremely difficult to focus on course work. Most colleges provide services from licensed professional counselors or psychology graduate students under the supervision of a licensed professional psychologist. Don't hesitate to seek help when you suspect your emotional state is suffering. Campus counseling services

vary in cost; many are free for a limited number of individual or group sessions. If you cannot find the services you need on campus, ask for a referral to a licensed practitioner in your community.

What Is "Academic Integrity" All About?

Academic integrity is fundamental to the mission of higher education. You are expected to do your own work and to prevent others from stealing your work. Failure to do so undermines learning, compromises a healthy personal value system, and can sometimes lead to the temptation to engage in other immoral or illegal activities. You should always resist the temptation to cheat, and avoid association with anyone who does cheat or suggests getting involved in cheating behavior.

The penalties for cheating or plagiarism can be severe, ranging from receiving a zero for the course to suspension or expulsion from the university. Make sure you understand your university's definitions and regulations regarding cheating and plagiarism.

Forms of cheating include, but are not limited to, copying answers from another student's exam; bringing unauthorized notes or materials into an exam; stealing exam materials from a university office; collaborating with other students on homework or exams (unless the instructor specifically permits it); or copying another student's homework assignment. You may also be subject to penalty if you fail to keep your homework and term papers secure, thus allowing another student to copy them. Double submission, or turning in the same paper in two different courses, is also usually considered to be academic dishonesty.

The term "plagiarism" refers to the act of copying another person's work and passing if off as your own, or, using another person's ideas without properly crediting the source. Examples of plagiarism include, but are not limited to, submitting another student's work; copying or purchasing papers from the Internet; or using materials from any source (books, articles, magazines, lectures, the Internet) without proper citations.

The Internet has a wide range of sites offering to sell you term papers on any subject under the sun. But don't be tempted. There are also sites that faculty members use to compare your paper with term papers on the Internet! Faculty are very aware of the temptations to copy material from the Internet, and they can quickly and easily identify any text matches and the sources of those matches.

Failing to cite sources is a very easy mistake to make. When it's late and you are in a hurry to finish a paper, it is easy to forget the procedure for proper citation. In addition, some students do not fully understand the rules for proper citations.

Cheating is not a victimless crime . . . see the box below for some thoughts on the damage it causes.

How Cheating Hurts Everyone

It Hurts Individuals

✗ **Cheating sabotages academic growth.**
Because the grade and the instructor's comments apply to someone else's work, cheating makes accurate feedback impossible.

✗ **Cheating sabotages personal growth.**
Educational accomplishments inspire pride and confidence. What confidence will students have when their work is not their own?

✗ **Cheating can have long-term effects.**
Taking the easy way out in college may spill over into graduate school, jobs, and relationships. Would you want a doctor, lawyer, or accountant who had cheated on exams handling your affairs?

It Hurts the Community

✗ **Widespread cheating causes honest students to become cynical and resentful,** especially if grades are curved and the cheating directly affects other students.

✗ **Widespread cheating devalues a college degree.** Alumni, potential students, graduate students, and employers learn to distrust degrees from schools where cheating is widespread.

✗ **Widespread cheating creates an environment of mistrust.** Would you want to live in a community when you doubt the integrity of its citizens?

Here are a few tips to help keep you out of trouble:

- If you are expected to cite sources in your written work, make sure you understand exactly what style guide (i.e., APA, Turabian, or MLA) your instructors expect you to use, and follow it closely.
- If you study with friends for exams, do not sit next to each other during the exam. Similar essay answers or a similar pattern of multiple-choice or short-answer responses may prompt the professor to suspect copying.
- Do not do schoolwork for your friends or give copies of your work to your friends. If you ask a friend to simply turn in an assignment for you, put it in a sealed envelope and sign your name, with the date, across the seal.
- Do not leave homework assignments or term papers sitting out where roommates or friends can access and copy them.
- Keep your computer files password protected, or do not allow others to use your computer.
- Give yourself enough time to complete writing assignments. Rushed work is prone to missed or sloppy citations.
- Don't associate with students who cheat or plagiarize.

For further information regarding academic integrity and the policies at your school, contact your Student Conduct or Judicial Affairs office, or contact your academic advisor.

? Questions for Class Discussion

1. So far, does school seem more difficult than at your previous school? Why or why not?
2. Many students today find mathematics courses more difficult than other subjects. Why do you suppose this is so?
3. Many students who have the best intentions to complete college end up dropping out. What are some of the reasons this happens?
4. Why do some students cheat?
5. What can be done on your campus to reduce cheating?
6. Do you intend to adopt the 3RM method? Why or why not?

Activity

Academic success often means taking advantage of campus resources that can help you. If you have difficulty, don't wait until it's too late to seek assistance. Next to each item below, write down the office address and telephone number of each campus resource. If you cannot find it, ask your advisor—perhaps it is identified by another name at your school.

Resource	Office Address	Telephone
Main Library		
Academic Advising		
Financial Aid Office		
Tutoring Services		
Campus Police		
Counseling Services		
Health Clinic		
Career Services		
Registrar		
Other		

Journal Assignment

Adopting effective study skills requires self-discipline and commitment to your academic goals. Reflect on your level of confidence in your current study skills. Write one to two pages. To direct your writing, consider and answer these questions:

1. Do I believe that I have the necessary study skills to achieve my academic goals?
2. If not, where is improvement needed?
3. What distracts me when I should be studying?
4. What can I do to minimize distraction and focus on academics?

Summary

- Transfer students often find the level of academic expectations to be quite different at their new institution.
- Students can improve their study skills by using the "3RM" method.
- Regular attendance and good lecture notes are essential to success.
- Math courses often pose a particular challenge; be sure to use all the resources you can to master the level of mathematical competency required for your degree.
- Students can adopt strategies for effective test taking.
- Take care to avoid academic misconduct.
- Know where to turn for help on campus.

Case Study

Laura had decided to attend the community college in her small hometown for the first two years, live with her parents, work to save money, and get her "basics" out of the way. She planned to earn her associate's degree and then transfer to a four-year school. Laura was a very organized person. She worked 20 hours per week at the espresso shop in the evenings, hung out with friends on the weekends, and still managed to maintain nearly a perfect grade point average. Laura had decided that she would like to go on to dental school following completion of her bachelor's degree, and had carefully followed the proper curriculum for admission to several dental programs in her region.

Laura was very excited to transfer to Western University, a large school of over 20,000 students. One of her friends from high school, Cindy, was already attending Western, and offered Laura a room to rent in Cindy's house off campus. Laura felt very confident that with two years of college already successfully completed, and a good friend to help her get adjusted to her new school, the final two years of college should be no trouble at all.

When Laura arrived at Western, she quickly began looking for a new part-time job. She knew she would have to work consistently in order to pay the higher tuition at Western. She found an evening and weekend position in a coffee house near campus, and was pleased to learn that they could offer her up to 30 hours per week. Laura had worked only 20 hours per week previously, and managed to maintain good grades with free time to spare, so she took up the manager's offer. After all, with her expenses on the rise, she knew she could use the extra money.

The next day, Laura met with an academic advisor to register for classes. Laura explained that she planned to apply to dental school, and the advisor helped Laura to enroll in the proper science courses. Laura and her advisor crafted a long-term plan of study that would ensure graduation in four semesters, including all of the prerequisites for dental school. Laura noted that there were a lot of science courses yet to take—most with labs—but she had aced biology as well as first-year chemistry and felt confident she would continue to do well.

Laura knew what it meant to be a dedicated student. She knew from experience how many hours she had to commit to study outside of class. She made sure to set aside the study time she believed she needed.

At mid-term, Laura was crushed to learn she was earning less than a C average. Her plans for dental school were in jeopardy. *She had been devoting the same amount of time to her studies as she had before*, but somehow it just wasn't nearly enough. Her added work hours left her no time at all for friends. Laura felt very discouraged.

Food for Thought

Which of William Bridges' phases of transition does Laura find herself in at this time? What was the critical error in judgment that Laura made? What can she do now to fix the problem?

Study Skills II

4

> New knowledge is the most valuable commodity
> on earth. The more truth we have to work with,
> the richer we become.
>
> —Kurt Vonnegut

In a Student's Voice

"I feel that two-year colleges and four-year universities are totally different; especially the education method. Like at the community college, I felt that all the material was spoon-fed. But here, whatever material you need to know, you need to do it yourself. I mean, they just teach you very briefly, but the homework, or the lab, or whatever, is always very detailed. You need to spend time reading outside of class, or whatever, before you can even do your homework."

—Jill, transfer student
(Nowak, 2004)

Learning Objectives

- Understand the skills needed for upper-division course work
- Learn the process and goals involved in critical thinking
- Recognize errors in logic
- Distinguish between fact and opinion
- Learn how to become a creative thinker
- Become familiar with the process and expectations involved in research writing

Quick Start Quiz

Assess your existing knowledge of key components of this chapter. Check each item below that applies to you:

❑ I can describe some of the differences between lower-division and upper-division course work.
❑ I understand why it is important to become a critical thinker.
❑ I can think creatively when needed.
❑ I know how to use the main library on my campus.
❑ I am familiar with the process and expectations involved in research writing.

How Will My Course Work Here Be Different?

During your first year or two in college, it is likely that most of your courses have been freshman and sophomore level—what is generally referred to as "lower-division" course work. You may now be ready, or will soon be ready, for junior- and senior-level courses, or "upper-division" course work. The academic expectations are usually much different in upper-division courses, and the cognitive skills that you need to be successful are more complex than those you may have found adequate for success in previous college courses. You may also find the nature of your assignments has changed as a function of the differing size and mission of your new school. In this chapter, we'll introduce the types of skills that you will need to master in order to be successful in many upper-division courses, as well as some of the more challenging tasks involved in upper-division course assignments.

Bloom's Taxonomy, developed by Benjamin Bloom in 1956, described a framework for arranging cognitive skills in order of their complexity. As you can imagine, we master basic skills early in our lives and progress to more complex types of skills as our intellectual development continues. Bloom's hierarchy begins with *knowledge* as the base, then moves to *comprehension, application, analysis, evaluation,* and finally concludes with *synthesis* at the top. Each level represents a more complex manner of learning. Professors may draw upon this framework as they develop learning objectives for their courses, using higher-level skills in junior- and senior-level courses. You may find that you will be asked to draw upon these skills in both written assignments and on exams. For this reason it is important to understand what specific behaviors are expected in each of these categories. We'll discuss each of these types of skills in more detail.

- Knowledge (memorizing). This is the most basic of skill levels. To demonstrate knowledge of a fact or idea simply involves repeating that fact or idea as it was originally learned.
- Comprehension (understanding). To demonstrate comprehension, a student must explain or interpret an idea, or compare and contrast one idea

with another. Exam questions may include the words *explain, discuss, summarize, illustrate, compare,* or *contrast.*

- Application (using). Application skills involve transferring and using your knowledge to a new situation or in a real-life context. Exam questions might include words such as *demonstrate, apply, complete, relate,* or *construct.*
- Analysis (taking apart). When we analyze something, we break it down into its component parts and look for elements, patterns, and organization and relate them to one another. Key words to look for on exam questions include *analyze, categorize, organize, classify,* or *deconstruct.*
- Evaluation (judging). To evaluate something is to assess or critique based on a specific set of criteria. Exam questions that ask for an evaluation might include the words *assess, critique, evaluate, decide, recommend, explain,* or *support.*
- Synthesis (putting together). A task involving synthesis will require the student to create a proposal, product, or idea that is new. Ideas from various sources will be drawn together. Your professor is looking for synthesis when he or she uses terms such as *create, develop, generate, design, construct,* or *compose* (Andreatta, 2006).

As you study, try to ensure that you understand the material at as many levels as you can. Developing this habit will help you to be prepared for any type of exam question that comes your way.

What Is "Critical Thinking" and Why Do I Care?

Critical thinking is a term you may have heard before. It is a skill that we all need to develop for success in college as well as life beyond college as responsible citizens, parents, neighbors, and workers. Critical thinking helps us to develop informed opinions and attitudes about the important issues and events that shape our lives. But what exactly is critical thinking?

None of us is born a critical thinker. As children, we accept as truth what authority figures tell us. Our parents may have told us that Santa Claus would come on Christmas Eve, but only after all of the children are in bed. Our elementary school teachers may have told us that Christopher Columbus discovered America in 1492. We generally did not question these matters. But as we grow and mature, we do not assume everything we see, read, and hear is accurate. We begin to ask a lot of questions. Furthermore, as citizens of the Information Age, we are now keenly aware of the significant amount of unreliable information labeled as fact. It is often the case that the same set of circumstances, the same set of facts, will produce widely divergent sets of opinions. We must ask questions to help us determine the truth, establish educated opinions, and make informed choices. As a college student, you will ask a great deal of questions, and thoughtful questioning is a key characteristic of a critical thinker.

Critical thinking helps us to detect prejudice and bias, illogical conclusions, or outright deception. Critical thinking helps us to question our own assumptions and become open to a change of opinion when evidence warrants. Critical thinking plays a vital role in social change, and is fundamental to the survival of a democracy. Critical thinking is a process that helps us to "figure things out" via thoughtful judgment and evaluation. So how does one become a critical thinker?

The process of learning to think critically should begin with four basic questions: Why, Who, What, and How. Let's work through an example. You've just picked up your school newspaper and see an editorial written by a fellow student at your college. The editorial is entitled, "No More Football!" and goes like this:

> "College athletics should be abolished. College athletics are a constant source of corruption, wasted resources, and wasted time, and serve only to undermine the academic mission of our university. The term 'student athlete' is an oxymoron! Student athletes are not interested in being students. They take the easiest courses in the easiest majors, are coddled by their professors, and receive high grades they do not deserve, all while receiving free tutoring that the nonathlete, serious students do not receive. Their classes are scheduled around practice schedules and they are excused from missing classes on away-game weekends. To add insult to injury, our athletes are idolized by students, faculty, and staff as if they are somehow superior to other students.
>
> In addition, all students are required to pay athletic facility fees whether or not they ever go to a game. This is wrong! If I am a serious student who does not endorse athletics, then my tuition and fees should go toward academics. Administrators continually seek funding from alumni to further enhance our athletic programs when they should be seeking funding to enhance academics. How can we call ourselves an institution of higher learning when our money, our time, and our attention all go to athletics? Academics or athletics? Which do you choose?"

Let's now engage the critical thinking process!

- *Why:* Ask yourself why the issue is important. You may be an avid college sports fan; you may agree with the editorial and wonder if the attention to athletics has gone too far; or you may be concerned about recent hikes in tuition and fees and would like to learn more about where your hard-earned money may be going. You are certainly aware that college sports are deeply entrenched in our culture; would that or could that ever change? Would such a change be in the best interests of our culture and the individuals involved?

- *Who:* Who wrote the editorial? We may assume the author is not an athlete, but do we know for sure? Does he or she have any direct experience or knowledge of the athletic program? For example, an intern in the athletic director's office might carry more credibility than a student with no interest in or experience with sports. Everybody has an opinion, but not all opinions are necessarily of equal value. Question the source.

- *What:* What are the various points of view on the topic? It would be interesting to survey a variety of people on campus. Imagine calling a meeting with the author of the editorial, a student athlete, the athletic director, the chief academic officer, your history professor, a student affairs staff member, and you. Each person will bring different perspectives, different values, and different experiences to the table. If you were to attend this meeting, your mission would be to listen carefully to everything that is said with an open mind, be tolerant of differing opinions, and identify each person's assumptions.

- *How:* How well is each viewpoint from your friends and neighbors supported? Clearly the editorial above does not include data or supporting evidence, just assertion after assertion. The assertions may be true or mostly true, but without factual support they lack credibility. What evidence do others provide? What evidence do you see? How might you gather further information on the topic?

Careful consideration of the issue from all angles, along with identification of supporting or discrediting evidence, will help you to critically analyze the editorial's assertions and to discover your own valuable and valid stand on the issue.

What About Logic?

Critical thinkers are logical thinkers. One way to strengthen your critical thinking skills is to learn to identify errors in logic. Such errors are called *fallacies*. Here are five fallacies that you will want to learn to recognize and avoid in your thinking:

- *Drawing conclusions with little evidence:* Stereotyping or making generalizations are examples of drawing conclusions in situations when we do not have all of the necessary information. In the example above, "No More Football," the author asserts that "student athletes are not interested in being students." Did the author survey student athletes to determine if indeed this statement is accurate? If so, no evidence is presented. This assertion may be made on the basis of interactions with a very limited number of student athletes, or perhaps even mere speculation.

- *Appealing to emotions:* Many fallacious arguments are based on key emotions that humans respond to, such as fear, patriotism, or envy. For example, if I am running for President of the United States, and I film a commercial in which I wave the flag and shout, "Vote for me! It's the American thing to do!" I am appealing to my audience's sense of patriotism but have presented no definition of what "American" means in this context, nor have I provided any data to support the statement.

- *Ad hominem* attacks: This is essentially name-calling or an attack on someone's character as a means to diminish that person's credibility. Let's say the city mayor and the high school principal are debating the merits of school vouchers. The principal makes his point, and in response the mayor calls the principal a thoughtless elitist. Unless the mayor specifically refutes the points the principal has made, he has created a fallacious argument.

- *Appealing to authority:* You see examples of this type of fallacy every day. Where? Advertising! The next time you see a famous celebrity or athlete endorse a product on television, you will know that the advertiser is appealing to authority. Rather than provide actual evidence of the usefulness of the product, advertisers depend on consumers believing the product is good because someone famous says so.

- *False dilemma:* If you are presented with two choices, when in reality there are more than two choices, you are faced with a false dilemma. There may very well be a third or fourth solution to a problem, but the argument omits those options. In "No More Football," the author presents a false dilemma toward the end of the essay. The phrase "academics or athletics" suggests that there are only two positions on the subject and that there is no middle ground. There could very well be a third alternative, such as increasing fundraising efforts in academics to match the levels of funding in athletics.

Fact or Opinion: How Do I Tell the Difference?

Sometimes it is difficult to tell whether or not a statement is a fact, or simply the author's opinion. Critical thinking requires distinguishing between the two. When an argument is based upon fact, it is usually more credible and logical. When an argument is based on opinion, it is simply one person's attitude toward the issue and may or may not be or become true. Here are some guidelines:

Fact-based statements:

- Describe what "is" rather than what "ought to be"
- Are testable or measurable
- Are verifiable
- Can be proven true or false

Opinion-based statements:

- Are based on someone's personal attitudes or values
- Suggest what "ought" to be
- Are based on assumptions
- Are speculations, predictions, or guesses (Koch and Wasson, 2002)

For example, consider this statement: "Females perform better academically at my college than males." Fact or opinion? This statement could very well be a fact if you collect grade point average data from both genders and the resulting correlation supports the statement. Of course you would want to be very specific in terms of the period of time and specific population being measured, but in general the statement is testable. Now consider this statement: "Females will eventually surpass males in managerial and executive positions." Even with data, such as a 20-year trend showing women catching up to men, this statement is mere speculation of a future event, and for now is an opinion. A more realistic statement might be, "Data collected over the past 20 years suggest that females will eventually surpass males in managerial and executive positions."

As you can see from this process, critical thinking is an important habit to establish as you encounter ideas that may be new to you, or ideas and perspectives that are different from your own. If you evaluate new evidence thoroughly and conclude that your existing viewpoint is still valid, then you have made an educated and informed choice about your stand on the issue. However, after considering new evidence you may conclude that your perspective is no longer valid. When you are willing to thoughtfully consider what you believe, you have embraced the ethic of tolerance, open-mindedness, and willingness to change that is the hallmark of an educated, thoughtful, and enlightened person. This is a profound and essential purpose of your college education.

Activity

Based on the guidelines for separating fact from opinion, identify the fact-based statements below with an F and the opinion-based statements with an O:

_____ 1. College students should not own pets.
_____ 2. Middle-school children watch more television than any other age group.
_____ 3. Obese people are unattractive.
_____ 4. Men under 25 have more automobile accidents than men over 25.
_____ 5. Good citizens always vote.
_____ 6. Smokers are more likely to get lung cancer than nonsmokers.
_____ 7. Global warming will cause an increase in bad weather over the next 10 years.

___ 8. High school students who play chess every week have better analytical skills than students who do not play chess.

___ 9. Blondes have more fun.

___ 10. Workers who take at least 10 days of vacation each year have higher levels of job satisfaction.

Flip to the end of the chapter for the answers!

Can I Be a Creative Thinker?

Have you ever had an assignment that called for a new idea, or a creative solution to an old problem? Do you ever have trouble coming up with ideas? Does it seem to take forever? You can expect future assignments as well as exam questions to tap your creative juices, so it is useful to have a strategy for creating new ideas in place. In this segment we'll talk about the process of creative thinking, and offer some strategies to help make the process easier and fun, too!

- The first step to fueling creativity is to *relax.* If you are feeling anxious or worried, creative thought comes much more slowly. Before tackling a project that calls for creativity, find a peaceful place, take deep breaths, and thoroughly relax your body and mind.

- *Break the rules.* In *A Whack on the Side of the Head,* Roger von Oech describes several barriers to creative thinking that he calls "mental locks." Mental locks are attitudes or experiences that prevent you from coming up with new ideas. For example, you may have heard in the past that there is one "right answer." Consequently we are mentally programmed to think that only one solution is the correct one and it comes from someone else (i.e., the teacher). Additionally, humans are creatures of habit. This can be a good thing as we go about our daily routines—especially if we foster good habits such as brushing our teeth after every meal or exercising every day—but habitual thinking can keep us from thinking differently about a problem. To enhance your creativity, try to break the rules; think outside of the box.

- Next, *brainstorm.* When you are trying to find a solution to a problem, try to jot down as many related ideas as you can. You might involve friends or classmates in the process. Write everything down. Even the most outlandish ideas warrant consideration—sometimes crazy thoughts foster related thoughts that become more realistic.

- Create *idea cards.* Great ideas may pop up at any time—so be prepared! Your brainstorming sessions will set the wheels in motion, and more ideas or solutions may occur to you later. You'll want to keep a set of 3 x 5 index cards (or perhaps a small notebook) in your book bag so that you can jot down new ideas whenever they occur. Have you ever awakened from a dream with a great idea? Your subconscious is often at work while you're asleep! Consider setting your idea cards along with a pen on your nightstand, too.

- Finally, be aware of emotional blocks to creativity. Always tell yourself *I am creative*. When you tell yourself you're not creative, it becomes a self-fulfilling prophecy. Fostering your creative side will help in many academic situations, and may also come in handy in your personal life. You may find the guidelines in this segment useful in many situations outside the classroom. What problems can you think of in your life that could use a fresh, creative solution?

See the box below for more ways to boost your creative efforts!

TAKE CHARGE

Of Your Imagination

If you accept the proposition that everyone has the potential to be creative, this means you, too! But you may need to rethink your environment to promote a more creative style. Here are some simple ideas to experience greater creativity on a day-to-day basis.

- **Decorate your door or bathroom mirror.** Find images, cartoons, headlines, and pictures that express who you are and put them up. The images will express to others your personality and values. You may generate some conversation with new acquaintances based on what images you post. The images can also remind you of your commitment to live a more creative life.

- **Use a thesaurus.** When writing, come up with new words that may have a stronger impact on your readers.

- **Use titles with pizazz.** Don't settle for a mundane introduction to work that you have written. Imagine what ideas might be most captivating. Devote some time to helping your work stand out.

- **Sit in a different place.** Unless you are restricted by a seating chart, move around in classes or in the lunch room. Humans are creatures of habit. Break your habit. It may produce new perspective and new friends.

- **Think "connections."** Explore how what you are learning in one class might inform what you are learning in another. These connections may provide you with some novel insights that you can share during class discussion.

- **Go with your second impulse.** Your first impulse is likely to represent an easier path, perhaps arising from routine ways that you approach problems. Go with an approach that is less characteristic of your style.

How Can I Become a Better Writer?

Many of your upper-division courses may include a writing component. You may notice a lengthy paper due at the end of the semester or quarter, or a series of shorter papers due throughout the term. A research paper will require you to do a significant amount of reading on the topic of your choice, assimilate the information that you have gathered, organize it meaningfully and clearly, and develop conclusions of your own based on what you have learned. Your professor will usually specify a minimum number of pages, say five to ten to fifteen or more, and may also specify a minimum number of sources that you are expected to cite. If the paper will be a lengthy one or if you want to seek out additional assistance or feedback for your work, be sure to begin working on it early in the academic term. A well-written paper cannot be completed in a day or two. One of the most important guidelines for writing college papers is to follow your professor's instructions carefully, and seek clarification of anything that you do not understand. Often term papers comprise a substantial portion of the final grade for the course.

Selecting a Topic

Your professor may assign a topic for your paper, or he or she may ask you to identify your own topic related to the course content. If you are to select your own topic, be sure to select one that interests you! It sounds silly but is an important consideration. Because you are going to be spending a fair amount of time working on this project, selecting a topic that bores you will certainly compromise your motivational level, your effort, your learning, and ultimately your grade.

Second, it is critical to refine your topic to one that is neither too broad nor too narrow for the length of your paper. If you choose a topic that is too broad, your paper will not be sufficiently detailed. If your topic is too narrow, you may cover it in fewer pages than your assignment requires. It is always a good idea to discuss your topic with your professor as you narrow it down so that you arrive at a manageable scope.

Developing Your Thesis Statement

When you have selected your topic you are ready to develop the thesis statement. A thesis statement is a sentence that states the main idea of the paper. In the beginning, your thesis statement will be a "working thesis." It may be broad at first. As you collect information related to your topic, you will refine your thesis statement to reflect the material that you will cite in your paper.

For example, let's say you would like to research the impact of technology on college student development. Your working thesis might be something like this: "The advent of modern technology, such as electronic mail and cellular telephones, has impacted student development." As you do your research, the information you collect may help you to refine the statement to something more specific, like this: "The proliferation of the cellular telephone has inhibited the development of college student autonomy by enabling and encouraging continued dependence on parental guidance."

Selecting Sources

Depending on the nature of the course and the topic you select or are assigned, your sources may need to be "scholarly" sources—that is, these sources must be academic articles that you find in journals published by professional organizations. Scholarly sources differ from popular press sources in several ways. First, they are often the result of primary research conducted by the author. Second, they are usually intended for a very specific audience made up of faculty and researchers in a specific discipline. Third, they typically contain lots of text, maybe some charts and graphs, but little color, and little if any advertising. Examples of scholarly journals include the *Journal of the American Medical Association; Newspaper Research Journal;* or *Behavioral Neuroscience.* Your university library may subscribe to these journals. In contrast, popular press magazines are those you might find for sale in retail bookstores and might appeal to a broad audience rather than to members of a narrow field or academic discipline. The information upon which the articles depend may or may not be based on any sort of scientific discipline. The author is likely to be more of a generalist than an expert in one field, and may have considerable bias toward a particular point of view. On the other hand, the articles may be entirely factual and present the situation in a straightforward way. You will know by employing the critical thinking exercise described earlier in this chapter. Titles such as *Newsweek, Psychology Today,* and *People* are included in what we call popular press publications.

Your Library and You

College libraries can be huge and intimidating. They may be large buildings with multiple levels and row upon row upon row of books on every floor. Students frequently try to avoid using the library for a variety of reasons—for example, not understanding how the library is organized, feeling shy about asking for help, or feeling overwhelmed by the sheer volume of material housed in the library.

It will be difficult to conduct research and write quality papers if you do not know how, or if you simply do not wish to use your college library. If you are not yet familiar with your library, mark your calendar this week to pay a visit. Call ahead and find out if you can arrange for a tour. As a new student to your school, you'll feel more comfortable now asking for assistance than a night or two before a major paper is due. Librarians are usually knowledgeable and friendly folks who are there to help you.

On Your Campus

This week, practice locating articles in scholarly journals. Visit your campus library, or access your library catalog electronically. Search for a recent article related to your academic major. If it is available in full text, print it out, or make a photocopy from the hard copy in the library. Read the article and note the elements and organization of the material. What conclusions were drawn? What recommendations for future research were made? Then scan the reference list for other recent and related articles. Obtain one or two of those and repeat the exercise. You're on your way to becoming an academic researcher!

If your assignment requires scholarly sources, your first task is to identify articles related to your topic. This will involve using your university library—either an in-person visit or a virtual visit, if you can call up electronic databases that your library subscribes to via the Internet. Electronic databases combine many journals into groups based upon discipline. Determine what general category your topic falls into—for example, social sciences, education, or humanities—and then begin your search. Narrow down your topic as much as you can to maximize the relevance of the matches you get. Use the Boolean operators discussed in Chapter 2.

Some of your matches may be "full-text" articles. This means that you can read the entire article online, and print it out if you like. If your article is not full text, you'll need to find out if your library subscribes to the journal in which the article is published, and if so, take a trip to the library to find the journal and photocopy the article. If your library does not subscribe to the journal that published the article, you may be able to obtain a copy via an interlibrary loan. This is a service that enables your library to mail or e-mail a copy of the article from another library that does subscribe to the journal.

As you collect your sources, you'll need to take notes. Many students find that creating a 3 x 5 index card for each source is an effective way to organize the material. As you read each article or book, take note of the main points made in the article. What questions did the author ask? What conclusions did the author draw? Then, make sure you have complete bibliographic information for each source. You'll need accurate and complete bibliographic information when it comes time to type your complete bibliography or reference list. On the back of the index card, jot down the author's name or names, the year, title, journal title, volume and issue numbers, and page numbers. Instructors may require students to adhere to the protocols of specific style guides, such as American Psychological Association (APA), Modern Language Association (MLA), or Turabian. Be sure to locate the proper style guide for the proper format of each entry on your list as well as citations within your text.

Creating an Outline

A good outline is critical to a well-organized paper. Because you've collected information from a variety of sources, it may feel overwhelming at first to try to tie everything together in a meaningful and coherent fashion. Your outline will be your road map to success. Just follow these steps and you will be on your way!

First, review your note cards. Identify the major themes and sort the cards accordingly. These major groups will become your major level of headings. Arrange them from the most general to the most specific. Then, identify the major points for each theme. This second level of headings contains the points that explain each statement in the top level. Finally, the third level contains specific facts or details that support the second level.

Writing the Paper

Now that you have an outline, it's time to begin writing. Your professor may have given you a preferred structure for your assignment. If not, most papers include an introduction, review of the literature, discussion, conclusion, and references. This format allows you first to tell your reader what your paper is about and why it is important; then to present the information you have researched; next to discuss the ideas presented; and finally to summarize your work and draw any conclusions or make recommendations. So that you can visualize the components and organization of a research paper, a sample abridged manuscript in APA style is included in Appendix B.

The introduction is your opportunity to "sell" your paper to your reader. A well-written introduction captures the reader's attention and motivates him or her to continue to read your paper. It helps the reader know what to expect and enables him or her to better comprehend your writing by developing mental questions that will be answered in the following pages of the paper. It is usually good practice to write the introduction last—you may not be able to predict exactly how the paper will develop at first. By writing the introduction last, all of your ideas are already detailed on paper and it is much easier to pull the important ideas together to create an effective preview of your paper.

The review of the literature is the section in which you describe, or "review," the main points of the articles and books you have selected to support your topic. It is important for the reader to know what research has already been completed on your topic, or what perspectives already exist. This creates a foundation for developing your own perspective. Once your foundation is established, you can progress logically to developing your own conclusions about the subject. Here are a few tips:

- Follow your outline. Present similar themes together; group opposing viewpoints separately.

- Be very careful to paraphrase the material you have read and to cite your sources appropriately; review the academic integrity information in Chapter 3. Paraphrasing means putting another author's ideas into your own words—and that means completely in your own words. If you use three or more consecutive words from a source, this material is considered a direct quote and will need quotation marks. Triple check your citations to make sure they are in place and accurate—your professor may charge you with plagiarism even when it occurs unintentionally.

- Use direct quotes extremely sparingly—only when the language used is particularly unique or profound, or when changing the wording significantly weakens the author's meaning or intent. Excessive use of direct quotes is to be avoided; it suggests a lack of thorough evaluation and assimilation of material, or even laziness. Rewriting ideas in your own words helps you to better learn and understand the material.

- Use effective transitional phrases between paragraphs. A transitional phrase helps to link the previous paragraph with the information in the upcoming paragraph, thus creating a smooth flow of ideas. Transitional phrases help the reader make connections. See the sidebar below for an example.

- Include several perspectives on your topic. If your thesis statement supports one point of view over another, you will have the opportunity to illustrate the weaknesses of the opposing viewpoint, thus supporting the conclusion you have made, in the discussion section. If you limit your material to one point of view, your paper becomes an opinion column rather than a research paper.

- Omit irrelevant information. Don't be tempted to pad your paper with material from every source you have researched. It is reasonable to expect that some of the material you have gathered may in the end not be relevant enough to include in your paper, given the scope of your final thesis statement. It is not wasted energy, but rather just a normal part of the process.

Writing Effective Transitions Between Paragraphs

Transitions, in the context of writing, are the words and phrases that help your writing flow smoothly from one paragraph to the next. Transitional phrases help link the ideas and create a logical progression of information. Organizing your material well is the first step. Then, be sure to connect each idea with the previous one. Here is an excerpt from a textbook that serves as an example:

> "Binocular disparity is a very powerful (and probably innate) determinant of perceived depth. Yet we can perceive depth even with one eye closed. Even more important, many people who have been blind in one eye from birth see the world in three dimensions. Clearly then, there are other cues for depth perception that come from the image obtained with one eye alone. These are the monocular depth cues.
>
> Many monocular depth cues have been exploited for centuries by artists and are therefore called pictorial cues. Examples include linear perspective, interposition, and relative size. In each case the eye exploits an optical consequence of the projection of a three-dimensional world upon a flat surface" (Gleitman, 1996, p. 161).

Notice how the phrase "monocular depth cues" in the last line of the first paragraph is repeated in the opening sentence of the second paragraph, thus creating a smooth transition from the first idea to the next.

The third component of your paper, the discussion section, allows you to describe the various perspectives that you have identified in your research, evaluate the strengths and limitations of each one, and lead up to a restatement of your thesis. In the discussion section, rather than simply describing what you have found in your research, you are now comparing the relative merits or findings of each article with one another. Remember Bloom's Taxonomy? Evaluation requires a high level of understanding. So give the material careful thought and consideration. Be sure to base your evaluations on facts presented in your research, not your opinion. Your final conclusion will support your refined thesis statement.

In the final segment of your paper, the summary, you will briefly restate the major points of your paper and the conclusion that you have drawn. You may also make recommendations, raise new questions, or create suggestions for further research.

Proofing and Revising

It is always a good idea to complete your paper well ahead of your deadline so that you will have plenty of time to proofread, edit, reorganize, and revise.

Proofread your paper by yourself to catch the major errors, and then ask a professor or responsible friend to proof it as well. When we read our own writing our brains know what to expect, and often these expectations cause us to skim over material rather than scrutinize it word by word, thus missing errors.

As you read, ask yourself lots of questions. Did I follow the assignment instructions completely? Does my paper make sense to my readers? Is it well organized and logical? Are the ideas fully explained and supported? Does the language flow smoothly? Are all of my sources cited? Do all of the text citations appear in the reference list and vice versa?

Finally, take advantage of your campus writing center if you have one. Writing centers typically are created to provide assistance for students with their writing assignments. You can expect an individual meeting with a tutor who will offer feedback on your paper in terms of structure, content, organization, grammar, and word choice. Do bring a copy of your assignment so that your tutor will know exactly what is expected of you. Do not expect this person to proofread or edit your paper. Generally writing center staff members are trained to *help you learn how to become a better writer* so that you can incorporate what you have learned into your own assignments. Think of them as coaches rather than editors.

? Questions for Class Discussion

1. Using Bloom's Taxonomy, identify what types of cognitive skills you have used in previous college course work. Are the academic expectations at your new school different from those at your previous school? If so, how?
2. Do you feel comfortable using your college library? If not, why not?
3. Are most people critical thinkers? Do we think critically in some situations and not in others? Discuss examples.
4. What is creativity? Why is it important?
5. Identify examples of each type of fallacy.
6. Do you enjoy writing term papers? If not, why not? What can you do to learn to enjoy writing papers?

Journal Assignment

Based on the critical thinking segment earlier in the chapter, reflect upon your own tolerance or acceptance of new or different ideas. Write one to two pages. To direct your writing, consider answering these questions:

1. What personal or social issue do I feel most strongly about?
2. How did I arrive at my opinion on the issue?

3. Am I open to differing perspectives concerning this issue? Why or why not?
4. What are the consequences of changing my stand on an issue that is very important to me?

Summary

- Bloom's Taxonomy is a framework for understanding progressively complex cognitive tasks.
- Critical thinking is an important skill in academic inquiry and research writing.
- Recognizing common fallacies can help you avoid errors in reasoning.
- Distinguishing between fact and opinion can assist in sound reasoning.
- Creative thinking is another skill that can assist in solving problems, creating new ideas, or finding a variety of new solutions to old problems.
- Understanding the process of researching and writing papers is a critical skill for upper-division courses and assignments.

Case Study

Jason's first year in college took place at a very large state school, where class enrollment often exceeded 300 students. Very few written assignments were given, and instead most courses required objective midterm and final exams graded by machine. Jason transferred to a much smaller liberal arts school prior to his sophomore year. He was pleased to find himself in classes of 25 to 30, where he could get to know his professors and classmates. The course assignments were much different as well—essay exams and term papers were more the rule than the exception. Jason understood that his writing skills would be key to his success in his new environment.

Jason's fall term sociology class requirements included a 10-page term paper, due near the end of the semester. The assignment was to thoroughly research a topic related to social problems of college students. The paper was to include recommendations for change based on data collected from scholarly sources and a comprehensive evaluation of the issue.

Jason was not at all sure what he would be interested in researching for this project, so he spent the first few weeks of the semester observing other students as he went about his daily routine. It did not take long for Jason to identify a topic that he found very interesting. Jason observed that several of the guys on his residence hall floor usually played computer games in the evenings. Jason did not enjoy computer games himself, and rejected any invitations to join in the computer games each evening. Jason knew several "computer nerds" in high school and was opposed to being labeled as such!

As the days went by, Jason noticed that the group of computer gamers were spending more and more time playing—they started earlier in the evening and stayed up later each night. By the end of the third week of class Jason never saw them in class or in the cafeteria. They hung out solely with each other and had no other friends or contacts. Jason became more and more troubled by this. The more he thought about it, the more he became convinced that computer games were inherently detrimental to people and society. He had discovered the ideal topic for his term paper.

Jason went to the library and found five scholarly journals related to his topic, including *Computers and Human Behavior, Journal of Human Computer Interaction,* and *Behavior and Information Technology*. He diligently searched for articles that exposed the dangers and negative consequences for computer gamers. He deliberately omitted any information that he found relating to social, economic, or personal benefits of computer gaming, as such material would weaken his argument. He did a search on the Internet for additional information regarding increased work or school absenteeism, chronic depression, and suicide among computer gaming addicts.

Jason had no trouble filling the requisite ten pages with evidence of the social evils of computer games. Jason concluded in his paper that use of computer games should be regulated by the government and violators fined and/or jailed. He was very satisfied with his work on the paper and expected a grade of "A" as well as the praise and admiration of his professor.

When the paper was graded and returned, Jason was shocked and dismayed to learn that he had earned a C minus. What had gone wrong?

Food for Thought

What instructions for this assignment did Jason fail to follow? Did he engage in principles of critical thinking as he prepared his paper? Why or why not?

Solutions

Fact or Opinion Activity: The odd numbers are opinion-based statements, and the even numbers are fact-based statements.

Managing Your Time

5

> *"You may delay, but time will not."*
> —Benjamin Franklin

In a Student's Voice

"For me, I think I'm slightly different again from most college students because most college students don't have a wife and a child to deal with. Not to deal with, to deal with on top of the school. So for me it's not really about school anymore. It used to be, everything used to be about school for me, right through high school and even when I was an exchange student because I was an exchange student my senior year at high school. Everything was about school, school, school. And then of course everything changed, perspectives changed, my mind has changed completely. It's all about making the best out of life for my family now."

—Mark, transfer student
(Nowak, 2004)

Learning Objectives

- Understand the relationship between time management, goals, and priorities
- Become aware of your use of your time each week
- Become aware of the most common and most costly time wasters
- Consider time management tools for your daily use
- Create a personalized semester, weekly, and daily time management plan
- Learn the causes and cures for procrastination

Quick Start Quiz

Assess your existing knowledge of key components of this chapter. Check each item below that applies to you:

- ❏ My goals and priorities are clearly reflected in how I use my time each day.
- ❏ I can identify pockets of my time that could be used more effectively.
- ❏ I have selected and used time management tools such as a calendar book or PDA.
- ❏ I engage in "multitasking" when and where appropriate.
- ❏ I understand the reasons for procrastination and try to avoid it.

Where Does the Time Go?

Effective time management is one of the most critical skills for success in college and in life. For many students, especially those with multiple commitments outside of school, creating sufficient time for all of life's demands is a daily challenge.

Have you ever said to yourself, "I just don't have enough time"? We all have the same amount of time available to us:

- 1440 minutes each day
- 24 hours each day
- 168 hours per week

How we choose to spend each moment of our lives greatly influences the degree of success that we achieve in each of our life roles. When you feel as though you do not *have* enough time for a task or an activity, it often means that you have chosen not to *make* time for that task. Raising children, managing a household, or going to college may seem like commitments that you have no choice about, but the truth is that all of those commitments involve choices that we make.

Managing time well includes being aware of our daily decisions regarding how we spend our time, and the willingness to take responsibility for those choices. In this chapter, we will discuss the relationship between life goals, priorities, and how we spend our time. When you've finished the chapter, you should have a workable plan for managing your time that reflects your personal and academic goals and priorities.

Why Is It So Hard to Say "No"?

It is difficult for busy people to focus on planned activities each day without deviation. Unexpected social opportunities or pressures from others can occur daily. Learning to say "no" is a challenge for many of us. When family or friends pressure us to commit to an unplanned activity, the guilt that we feel for saying "no" is often greater than the frustration we feel for putting off our planned tasks and goals for the day. For example, you may have dedicated a sunny spring Saturday afternoon to doing research in the library for a term paper that is due in two weeks, only to be pressured by your children to take them to the zoo or by an elderly neighbor to help her plant her flower garden. For many of us, it is hard to put our needs ahead of others. In these cases, don't feel pressured to respond immediately. Say, "Let me check my calendar and get back to you." Then, take time to check your calendar and think it over. Look at the next few days and decide if you can realistically afford to put off your school commitments for another day without sacrificing your priorities. If the answer is yes, be sure to write down exactly when you plan to do the work you are postponing. If the answer is "no," you might try to find a time in the coming weeks that you can devote to the other activities, and let your family or friends down gently by saying, "I have made a previous commitment that I cannot postpone today, but can (take you to the zoo/help you plant flowers/whatever it may be) a week from tomorrow (or whenever you can)." Reasonable people will respect your decision without undue disappointment.

Learning to say "no" does not always involve a tradeoff between school-related and nonschool-related activities. For example, while students are encouraged to become involved in extracurricular activities on campus, it is easy to become overinvolved at the expense of academics. Some students thrive on taking leadership roles in student organizations and do very well. Consequently, they may be asked by multiple organizations to join and help out. It is hard to say "no" when you are being complimented on your leadership and social skills! In these cases, you must carefully consider how much time you have for extracurricular activities, and be selective. Choose to participate in those activities that will offer you the greatest opportunities for experience related to your ultimate professional or academic goals. In other words, you want to ensure that there are adequate returns on your investment of time. If you must say no, try to recommend a friend or classmate who may be equally qualified for the job.

Take a moment to consider your goals in all of the areas in your life. Are some goals more important to you than others? If so, you would naturally devote more time to those tasks each week than others. Do your daily activities reflect your goals? If not, why not?

How Do I Spend My Time?

Sounds like an easy question to answer, but are you really aware of how you spend each hour of the day? Doing a weekly "time diary" is a helpful exercise that we can use to track how we spend each hour of our time for one week, and then to examine the results closely, keeping our goals and priorities in mind. The time diary helps us to identify pockets of wasted time—time that we could be using more productively.

A time diary should be used in conjunction with your stated goals and priorities. Does the way you spend your time reflect those goals and priorities?

The following example is for Mike. Mike is a student carrying 15 hours of course work. He also works 20 hours each week at a local cafe, volunteers at the community retirement home each Saturday, exercises four days a week, and spends time with his girlfriend, Anne, his best friend, Jim, and his dog, Max.

Mike states that his number-one priority is school—he intends to earn a 4.0 every semester. His second priority is work. Mike depends on his income from the restaurant to pay for most of his living expenses. Third, he tries to spend as much time as he can with Anne, his friends, and his dog. Mike diligently tracked his time for one week using the template in Appendix C. Let's see how he did:

My Number One Goal: *Earning a 4.0 GPA this semester*
  Priority Activity related to that goal: *study time, tutor time, reading time*
Secondary Goal: *Earning sufficient money to pay bills*
  Priority Activity related to that goal: *working at least 20 hours per week and doing a great job so that my boss will offer me a raise!*

	MON	TUES	WED	THURS	FRI	SAT	SUN
5 AM	Sleep	Sleep	Sleep	Sleep	Sleep	Sleep	Sleep
5:30	Sleep	Sleep	Sleep	Sleep	Sleep	Sleep	Sleep
6 AM	Walk Max	Walk Max	Walk Max	Walk Max	Walk Max	Sleep	Sleep
6:30	Work out	Shower/eat	Work out	Shower/eat	Work out	Sleep	Sleep
7 AM	Work out	Sociology reading	Work out	Sociology reading	Work out	Walk Max	Sleep
7:30	Shower/eat	Sociology reading	Shower/eat	Sociology reading	Shower/eat	Work out	Sleep
8 AM	Drive to campus	Sociology reading	Drive to campus	Sociology reading	Drive to campus	Work out	Sleep
8:30	Biology class	Drive to campus	Biology class	Drive to campus	Biology class	Shower/eat	Walk Max
9 AM	Biology class	Sociology class	Biology class	Sociology class	Biology class	Volunteer work	Shower/eat
9:30	Math class	Sociology class	Math class	Sociology class	Math class	Volunteer work	Drive to church
10 AM	Math class	Sociology class	Math class	Sociology class	Math class	Volunteer work	Church
10:30	Break	Advising appointment	Break	Biology lab	Break	Volunteer work	Church
11 AM	Math tutor	Lunch with Anne	Math tutor	Biology lab	Math tutor	Volunteer work	Drive home
11:30	Math tutor	Lunch with Anne	Math tutor	Biology lab	Math tutor	Volunteer work	Play with Max
12 PM	Lunch	Lunch with Anne	Lunch	Biology lab	Lunch	Lunch with friends	Lunch

12:30	English class	Study at library	English class	Lunch	English class	Lunch with friends	Watch football
1 PM	English class	Study at library	English class	Read for history	English class	Lunch with friends	Watch football
1:30	Drive home	Study at library	Drive home	Read for history	Drive home	Grocery shopping	Watch football
2 PM	Play with Max	History class	Play with Max	History class	Play with Max	Play with Max	Watch football
2:30	Check e-mail	History class	Check e-mail	History class	Check e-mail	Check e-mail	Watch football
3 PM	Study time	History class	Study time	History class	Study time	Internet poker	Watch football
3:30	Study time	Drive home	Study time	Drive home	Study time	Internet poker	Study time
4 PM	Study time	Check e-mail	Study time	Check e-mail	Study time	Wash car	Study time
4:30	Get ready/drive to work	Laundry	Get ready/drive to work	Internet poker	Get ready/drive to work	Get ready/drive to work	Study time
5 PM	Work	Laundry	Work	Internet poker	Work	Work	Study time
5:30	Work	Pick up dinner	Work	Eat/TV	Work	Work	Study time
6 PM	Work	Eat/TV	Work	Eat/TV	Work	Work	Dinner with Anne
6:30	Work	Eat/TV	Work	Study time	Work	Work	Dinner with Anne
7 PM	Work	Call Anne	Work	Study time	Work	Work	Dinner with Anne
7:30	Work	Call Anne	Work	Study time	Work	Work	Dinner with Anne
8 PM	Work	Call parents	Work	Out to movie with Jim	Work	Work	Dinner with Anne
8:30	Work	Study time	Work	Out to movie with Jim	Work	Work	Dinner with Anne
9 PM	Work	Study time	Work	Out to movie with Jim	Work	Work	Study time
9:30	Work	Study time	Work	Out to movie with Jim	Work	Work	Study time
10 PM	Drive home	Study time	Drive home	Out to movie with Jim	Drive home	Drive to Anne's house	Study time
10:30	Call Anne	Study time	Call time	Out to movie with Jim	Call Anne	Hang out with Anne	Study time
11 PM	Study time	Sleep	Sleep	Sleep	Sleep	Hang out with Anne	Study time
11:30	Study time	Sleep	Sleep	Sleep	Sleep	Hang out with Anne	Study time
12 AM	Sleep	Sleep	Sleep	Sleep	Sleep	Hang out with Anne	Sleep
12:30	Sleep	Sleep	Sleep	Sleep	Sleep	Hang out with Anne	Sleep
1 AM	Sleep	Sleep	Sleep	Sleep	Sleep	Hang out with Anne	Sleep
1:30	Sleep	Sleep	Sleep	Sleep	Sleep	Drive home	Sleep
2 AM	Sleep	Sleep	Sleep	Sleep	Sleep	Sleep	Sleep
2:30–4:30 AM	Sleep	Sleep	Sleep	Sleep	Sleep	Sleep	Sleep

How did Mike spend his time?
Sleep: 48 hours
Study/reading/tutoring time: 26 hours
Employment: 20 hours
In class: 17 hours
Anne: 12 hours
Personal (eating, showering, shopping, laundry, church, and so on):
    12 hours
Travel time: 10.5 hours
Entertainment: 9.5 hours
Max: 6 hours
Exercise: 4 hours
Volunteer work: 3 hours
Total: 168 hours

Mike has done fairly well at keeping up with his stated priorities. Using our guideline for study time, with 15 credit hours this semester, Mike should be studying at least 30 hours per week. With only 26 hours this week, Mike is coming up a bit short.

Mike is not getting quite enough sleep, averaging fewer than seven hours per night, and frequently feels overtired toward the end of the day when at work or home studying. This circumstance affects his ability to achieve his top two goals. He hopes to add at least another 30 minutes of sleep each night, so that he is more alert and productive. Such a change contributes to his academic and employment goals.

Mike also hopes to be able to spend more time with Anne, but does not want to sacrifice time working or studying. Additionally, Anne has threatened to refuse to visit Mike's apartment if he does not clean his bathroom, so that task must be included each week as well.

Mike carefully scoured his weekly time diary for pockets of "wasted time." He quickly noticed the "break" between math class and math tutor on Mondays, Wednesdays, and Fridays. During that time he never did anything in particular, but rather wandered around campus, greeted friends, went to the espresso bar, or otherwise killed time waiting for his tutoring appointment. He decided that he could easily accomplish one important daily task during that time—reading and responding to his e-mail. He discovered a computer lab close to the tutor's office that he decided to use for this purpose.

Additionally, Mike noticed he spent two full hours during his week playing Internet poker. This activity did not help him achieve any of his goals, so Mike decided to eliminate this activity altogether.

Next, Mike tried to find room in his week to spend more time with Anne. He did not want to eliminate time with his best friend Jim, or completely eliminate time for himself, so Mike began to think about "multitasking"—involving Anne with some of his activities that she would also enjoy or find productive, such as walking the dog, having lunch with friends, or studying.

Finally, Mike wanted to find more time for sleep. By inviting Anne to come by to walk the dog with him in the afternoon, rather than walking Max by himself in the morning, Mike accomplished two goals: thirty extra minutes of sleep in the mornings, and more time with Anne.

Mike is making positive changes. Although his weekly routine was quite productive already, Mike has identified new ways to improve with some relatively minor schedule adjustments. He has identified the activities that waste his time and do not contribute to his goals. By eliminating some or all of those wasted hours, Mike has increased his sleep time, study time, and time with Anne, and—last but not least—Mike now spends 30 minutes each week cleaning his bathroom!

Here is Mike's new "ideal" weekly calendar. The shaded cells indicate a change from the original time diary:

Let's examine Mike's new plan!

	MON	TUES	WED	THURS	FRI	SAT	SUN
5 AM	Sleep	Sleep	Sleep	Sleep	Sleep	Sleep	Sleep
5:30	Sleep	Sleep	Sleep	Sleep	Sleep	Sleep	Sleep
6 AM	Sleep	Sleep	Sleep	Sleep	Sleep	Sleep	Sleep
6:30	Work out	Shower/eat	Work out	Shower/eat	Work out	Sleep	Sleep
7 AM	Work out	Sociology reading	Work out	Sociology reading	Work out	Sleep	Sleep
7:30	Shower/eat	Sociology reading	Shower/eat	Sociology reading	Shower/eat	Work out	Sleep
8 AM	Drive to campus	Sociology reading	Drive to campus	Sociology reading	Drive to campus	Work out	Sleep
8:30	Biology class	Drive to campus	Biology class	Drive to campus	Biology class	Shower/eat	Clean bathroom
9 AM	Biology class	Sociology class	Biology class	Sociology class	Biology class	Volunteer work	Shower/eat
9:30	Math class	Sociology class	Math class	Sociology class	Math class	Volunteer work	Drive to church
10 AM	Math class	Sociology class	Math class	Sociology class	Check e-mail	Volunteer work	Church
10:30	Check e-mail	Advising appointment	Check e-mail	Biology lab	Check e-mail	Volunteer work	Church
11 AM	Math tutor	Lunch with Anne	Math tutor	Biology lab	Math tutor	Volunteer work	Drive home
11:30	Math tutor	Lunch with Anne	Math tutor	Biology lab	Math tutor	Volunteer work	Walk Max

12 PM	Lunch	Lunch with Anne	Lunch	Biology lab	Lunch	Lunch with Anne & friends	Lunch
12:30	English class	Study at library	English class	Lunch	English class	Lunch with Anne & friends	Watch football
1 PM	English class	Study at library	English class	Read for history	English class	Lunch with Anne & friends	Watch football
1:30	Drive home	Study at library	Drive home	Read for history	Drive home	Grocery shopping	Watch football
2 PM	Study time	Histtory class	Play with Max	History class	Play with Max	Walk Max	Study with Anne
2:30	Study time	History class	Study time	History class	Study time	Study time	Study with Anne
3 PM	Study time	History class	Study time	History class	Study time	Study time	Study with Anne
3:30	Walk Max with Anne	Drive home	Walk Max with Anne	Drive home	Walk Max with Anne	Check e-mail	Study with Anne
4 PM	Walk Max with Anne	Walk Max	Walk Max with Anne	Check e-mail	Walk Max with Anne	Wash car	Study with Anne
4:30	Get ready/drive to work	Laundry	Get ready/drive to work	Walk Max with Anne	Get ready/drive to work	Get ready/drive to work	Study with Anne
5 PM	Work	Laundry	Work	Walk Max Anne	Work	Work	Study with Anne
5:30	Work	Pick up dinner	Work	Eat/TV	Work	Work	Study with Anne
6 PM	Work	Eat/TV	Work	Eat/TV	Work	Work	Dinner with Anne
6:30	Work	Eat/TV	Work	Study time	Work	Work	Dinner with Anne
7 PM	Work	Call Anne	Work	Study time	Work	Work	Dinner with Anne
7:30	Work	Call Anne	Work	Study time	Work	Work	Dinner with Anne
8 PM	Work	Call parents	Work	Out to movie with Jim	Work	Work	Dinner with Anne
8:30	Work	Study time	Work	Out to movie with Jim	Work	Work	Dinner with Anne
9 PM	Work	Study time	Work	Out to movie with Jim	Work	Work	Study time
9:30	Work	Study time	Work	Out to movie with Jim	Work	Work	Study time
10 PM	Drive home	Study time	Drive home	Out to movie with Jim	Drive home	Drive to Anne's house	Study time
10:30	Call Anne	Study time	Call Anne	Out to movie with Jim	Call Anne	Hang out with Anne	Study time
11 PM	Study time	Sleep	Sleep	Sleep	Sleep	Hang out with Anne	Study time
11:30	Study time	Sleep	Sleep	Sleep	Sleep	Hang out with Anne	Study time
12 AM	Study time	Sleep	Sleep	Sleep	Sleep	Hang out with Anne	Sleep
12:30	Study time	Sleep	Sleep	Sleep	Sleep	Hang out with Anne	Sleep
1 AM	Sleep	Sleep	Sleep	Sleep	Sleep	Hang out with Anne	Sleep

1:30	Sleep	Sleep	Sleep	Sleep	Sleep	Drive home	Sleep
2 AM	Sleep	Sleep	Sleep	Sleep	Sleep	Sleep	Sleep
2:30	Sleep	Sleep	Sleep	Sleep	Sleep	Sleep	Sleep
3 AM	Sleep	Sleep	Sleep	Sleep	Sleep	Sleep	Sleep
3:30	Sleep	Sleep	Sleep	Sleep	Sleep	Sleep	Sleep
4 AM	Sleep	Sleep	Sleep	Sleep	Sleep	Sleep	Sleep
4:30	Sleep	Sleep	Sleep	Sleep	Sleep	Sleep	Sleep

Sleep: 51 hours—now Mike gets 7.5 hours of sleep on weeknights

Study/reading/tutoring time: 30 hours—hooray!

Employment: 20 hours

In class: 17 hours

Anne: 19.5 hours (overlaps other categories by 10 hours)

Travel time: 9.5 hours

Personal (eating, showering, shopping, laundry, e-mail, and so on): 12 hours

Entertainment: 5.5 hours

Max: 6.5 hours

Exercise: 4 hours

Volunteer work: 3 hours

Total = 168 hours

Activity

Using the worksheets in Appendix C at the back of this book, list your primary goals and priorities. Consider academic, social, family, and personal goals.

Then, log your time for one week. You will probably want to carry the worksheets with you so that you can jot down your activities as the day goes on, rather than attempting to recall how your time was spent at the end of each day. At the end of the week, with your goals and priorities in mind, examine how you spent your time. Identify time wasters or unnecessary time spent on activities that do not support your stated goals. Circle or highlight these blocks of time.

Next, you will create your "ideal" weekly calendar. Before you begin, it helps to determine how much time it takes you to perform specific tasks. For example, although two hours spent outside of class for every hour spent inside of class is a guideline for allocating study time, some students may need more time, some students less time. Sit down with one of your textbooks and take note of the time it takes to read and comprehend 10 pages. Once you have a good sense of how much time you need for reading, it will be easier to allocate the appropriate blocks of time each day to keep up with your reading load. How much time does it take to type your papers or assignments? If you are prone to "hunting and pecking," consider a keyboarding course, or if you can afford it, send your drafts to a professional typing service.

How Can I Stop Wasting Time?

What do you regard as a waste of your time? There are many, many ways that we spend our time unwisely on a daily or weekly basis. Wahlstrom et al. (2003) identified these top five culprits:

- *Television*—No surprise there! Studies show that Americans spend more time watching television than any other leisure activity (Wahlstrom et al., 2003). With more channels available on cable than most of us can ever watch, and programming around the clock, television can be a continuous temptation and distraction. Setting viewing limits for yourself is a wise idea.

- *Commuting*—If you find yourself driving back and forth to campus, consider your options. Is there public transportation available? Is there someone in your neighborhood with whom you could carpool? By alternating drivers you could make use of half of your time—or more, depending on the number of riders—on the road. Is moving to housing within walking distance of campus feasible for you? Some students assume that on-campus housing is always more expensive than off-campus. When taking utilities, cable and Internet access charges, as well as gasoline and vehicle maintenance costs into consideration, you may find on-campus housing to be comparable in cost to off-campus living.

- *Excessive work hours*—Only about 20 percent of students at public, four-year universities do not take out loans and do not work (King, 1998). That means the vast majority of students must work and/or take out loans to pay for college. Most students take advantage of a combination of sources, including loans, scholarships or grants, and paid employment. Financial planning will be discussed in detail in a future chapter, but for now, if you are working more than 20 hours per week and attend school full-time, you may want to consider other forms of financial aid so that you can reduce your work hours. It is difficult to attain your academic goals when you are focusing so much of your time and energy on employment.

- *Partying*—There is no question that socializing with others and drinking alcohol is a well-entrenched aspect of college life. Unfortunately, there is a correlation between heavy drinking and poor grades. A more detailed discussion on this topic can be found in Chapter 7. In brief, if you choose to drink, set limits for yourself. Take stock of your goals and decide how much partying is beneficial for you.

- *Internet use*—While the Internet is a valuable tool for research, as well as a convenient source of information and entertainment, how much is too much? Expert opinions vary on this one, so you'll need to use your best judgment. Some people use the Internet rarely, if at all. Others spend hours at a time, every day. The purpose of Internet use varies widely between individuals as well. For example, are you using the Internet to research a paper for class, or spending hours logged on to "Facebook"? Bottom line: when time spent online begins to interfere with other more important goals and priorities in your life, then it is time to consider setting limits.

On Your Campus

This week, identify pockets of time that you have during the day on campus in between classes or other scheduled activities. How can you best use this time? Create a specific plan for maximizing your productivity. Ideas might include dropping by a computer lab to check e-mail; finding a quiet nook for study; or going to the campus recreation center for a quick workout.

What Kinds of Time Management Tools Are Out There?

It will be difficult, if not impossible, to create an effective time management plan without some type of calendar that you use and rely on every day. Your calendar will help you prioritize your daily, weekly, and monthly tasks, stay organized, and help you keep track of your progress toward your goals. But you have to use it! The calendar has to be one that suits you. There are more choices today than ever before, so you should carefully consider your lifestyle, your comfort with technology, and your budget as you decide which type of time management product to use. Here are a few of the options:

- *Traditional paper calendar book/day planner.* These are widely available and relatively inexpensive. A calendar book typically includes pages that are preformatted with room to write in your obligations for each hour of the day. University bookstores frequently sell simple paper planners for a reasonable price. Often they are preprinted with campus events, information, and deadlines. They may not, however, offer more than one format to choose from. For more choices in formats, sizes, and covers, you might want to shop around.
- *Hand-held electronic planners.* These devices are available from a variety of manufacturers under a variety of names, such as Palm Pilot, Pocket

PC, BlackBerry, and so on. Collectively, we refer to these gadgets as personal digital assistants, or PDAs for short. These devices may also contain other features in addition to a calendar, such as a name and address database, a note pad, a calculator, and a "to do" list. For a little more money, you can purchase a unit with more complex additional features, such as wireless Internet and e-mail access, a camera, or video and audio capability. In addition you might consider a "smartphone"—this is a cell phone with PDA functions included. It is beyond the scope of this chapter to go into detail about the differences between the devices available—and the technology changes rapidly—but if you are comfortable using electronic gadgets, have a need or desire for the added features and portability of a PDA, and have a bit more money to invest, you may want to research your options.

- *Software for your home computer.* If you happen to use Microsoft Office already, you know it includes Outlook, an e-mail and calendar program. If not, a quick Internet search for "calendar software" will result in dozens of products for purchase or free download. These electronic calendars usually mimic paper calendars with daily, weekly, or monthly view options. Calendar software can often be used in tandem with a PDA, should you choose to purchase one. It is possible to synchronize both databases, often with wireless technology. This way both your home computer and PDA stay up to date.

The Millennial Generation

You may have heard the term "Millennial Generation." This is a reference to the people born after 1981, who graduated from high school in the new millennium, or the 21st century. "Millennials," as they are often called, are said to differ in many respects from the generations born before them, namely Generation X (1962–1980) and the Baby Boomers (1945–1961). Many of these differences, including attitude, learning style, and relationship with parents may impact the Millennials' approach to higher education.

One of these critical differences is the Millennial Generation students' level of comfort and familiarity with technology. Unlike previous generations, Millennials have grown up with personal computers, the Internet, compact discs, MP3 players, DVDs, cell phones, PDAs, and more. Millennials have never seen LPs or 8-track players (unless those items are stashed in the parents' garage)! In contrast, generations before the Millennial used neither cell phones nor personal

continued

computers in college. Telephone calls were made on pay phones and assignments completed on typewriters. Those generations could not have imagined the power and speed of the Internet. All of this technological change impacts how the Millennial Generation approaches homework assignments, organizes time, communicates with friends, family, and faculty members, and spends their free time.

If you are a member of the Millennial Generation, you may well be blessed with skills, talents, and expectations regarding technology and ease of access to information that will serve you well in college. However, it is wise to understand and respect the varying levels of comfort with technology that your older classmates may have. If you are collaborating on a class project with older students, talk openly with them about your learning strategies and listen for their perspectives. If you are not a member of the Millennial Generation, try to keep an open mind to learning the new technologies. Your younger friends may be able to help. A certain level of competence may be required or preferred when you enter the world of work in the 21st century!

How Do I Create a Personalized Time Management Plan?

Once you have identified and purchased the best calendar system for your needs, it is time to put it to work.

To begin, consider this often-told story. A professor places a one-gallon jar on his desk. He then piles in about a dozen large rocks, which reach to the top of the jar. He asks the class "Is the jar full?" The class answers, "Yes!"

The professor reaches below his desk and pulls out a bag of gravel. He pours the gravel in on top of and between the big rocks, again reaching to the top of the jar. He asks, "Is this jar full?" The class is suspicious now, and answers, "Probably not!"

The professor nods and then reaches below his desk and pulls out a bag of sand. He pours it in on top of the gravel and rocks, and asks, "Is this jar full?" The class is unsure.

The professor then takes a pitcher full of water and pours the water in on top of the rocks, gravel, and sand, filling the jar to the brim. He asks, "What is the point of this?"

The point is this: *If you don't put the big rocks in first, you probably won't fit them all in* (Hallberg et al., 2004).

The "big rocks" in your life are your most important goals and priorities. You'll need to know exactly what those "big rocks" are as you begin to create your master calendar, and schedule those tasks first.

At the start of each semester, gather information such as a course syllabus for each of your classes, your work hours if you are employed, family responsibilities such as transporting children, and/or club meeting and event times if you are participating in student organizations. You may have other activities and tasks to consider as well. These are the types of things that may be your "big rocks." Enter in all of those types of commitments for each month of the semester on your calendar. Then, using your ideal weekly calendar that you created earlier in this chapter as a guide, begin filling in your calendar with all of the details of your week. Finally, create a "to do" list at the end of each day for the following day. Do you ever get that feeling that there is something you were supposed to do today but cannot recall what it is? You may find that your stress level diminishes when all of your obligations are clearly indicated either on paper or electronically and readily available for review. You will also enjoy checking all those boxes off on your "to do" list each day!

What About "Multitasking"?

You have probably heard and used this word before. Simply put, multitasking means doing more than one thing at a time. You've probably "multitasked" many times before. Examples include talking on the telephone while cooking a meal; watching television while text-messaging your friend; or eating a sandwich while driving to work.

Multitasking can help you accomplish more each day. In our sample time diary earlier in this chapter, Mike was able to incorporate multitasking by walking his dog with his girlfriend. Here are some ways you may be able to multitask in beneficial ways:

- Review class notes while waiting in line or riding the bus
- Work on homework or reading assignments while doing your laundry
- Catch up on TV while exercising on the treadmill

What do these combinations of activities have in common? One of the activities in each set *does not require your continuous, full attention*. In these examples those activities are riding the bus (someone else is doing the driving); laundry (the washer and dryer are doing the work); and jogging (one need not commit full attention to keeping the feet moving). Effective multitasking depends on choosing appropriate combinations of tasks. Here are some combinations of tasks to avoid:

- Talking on your cell phone while driving a car
- Watching television and reading a textbook
- Completing your math homework while in history class

In these examples, each activity does require continuous, full attention. By shifting your attention back and forth, you lose information and can potentially create danger for yourself and others. Multitasking can be beneficial, but you must be selective about the tasks you combine.

Why Do I Procrastinate?

Do you sometimes put off for tomorrow what should be done today? Many college students do, for a variety of reasons. Procrastination can be a major factor in poor academic performance, due to missed deadlines, sloppy work, or lack of preparation for exams. In this section we'll discuss some of the common reasons that students procrastinate, and offer strategies that you can employ to overcome this bad habit!

One of the most common reasons that students procrastinate is *to avoid feelings of inferiority or inadequacy.* Students may not be consciously aware of this fact, but it happens quite often. If you wait until the last minute to complete an assignment, or wait until the night before the exam to begin studying, it is rarely possible to do well no matter how intelligent one is. The procrastinator in this scenario may well believe that had adequate time been spent on the assignment, s/he would have done very well. In this case poor performance is blamed on lack of time or preparation, *not lack of ability.* With such an excuse in mind, the student is protected from feeling inadequate.

Another common reason that students procrastinate is *failure to plan ahead.* Students may have the best of intentions, but if a major assignment or exam comes as a surprise, once again there is insufficient time for attention to detail or thorough preparation. It is imperative that you effectively use a day planner or other calendar tool to log your assignment due dates and exam dates, plan your study agenda for the semester accordingly, check your day planner several times a day, and update as needed.

A third reason why students procrastinate is negative feelings toward the instructor. If you are feeling hostile toward your instructor due to assignments that you feel are unfair, tests that are exceptionally difficult, or even personality conflicts, you may feel very reluctant to focus your time and energy on preparation for that course. To avoid those angry feelings, or to indulge feelings of rebellion, students are often tempted to procrastinate.

Procrastination is habit-forming. Once you begin to put off your assignments or study time for today, the work that you must do tomorrow looms larger. Then, it is even more tempting to procrastinate because the task ahead is now even more unpleasant and time-consuming than before. With each day that you delay, the amount of time you have to dedicate to doing your best work diminishes. It is easy to feel overwhelmed and discouraged very quickly when you know that getting "caught up" will take more hours of your time than you have to spend. Additionally, when working at the eleventh hour, you often do not have access to outside assistance when problems or questions arise. You may feel overtired or rushed as well. These factors create an even more formidable obstacle to achieving academic success.

What to do? Here are a few tips to help you avoid procrastination:

- *Be honest with yourself.* It is very easy to rationalize our behavior and to create excuses for putting off our work. If you are a frequent procrastinator, you might want to have a heart-to-heart conversation with a friend or family member who knows you well. Sometimes others can point out behavioral realities that we fail to observe or prefer to avoid. It will be difficult to effect a meaningful change if you are living in denial of your behavior.

- *Identify the activities that promote your procrastination.* Many of us have favorite pastimes that we tend to engage in at the expense of academic commitments. Or sometimes we spend more time than necessary at certain tasks. Common suspects are e-mail, telephone calls, television, or computer games. Once you've identified the activities that are keeping you from your school work, make a plan to eliminate or minimize time spent on those activities.

- *Create a daily and weekly "to do" list.* In conjunction with your calendar and established due dates and exam dates, be sure to set daily goals and stick to them. Be realistic with your goals so you avoid frustration if you cannot accomplish them all.

- *Include rewards for accomplishing your weekly goals.* Checking off all of the boxes on your "to do" list is satisfying in itself, but you might want to think about small ways to reward yourself and thereby provide a "guilt-free" incentive for a job well done.

- If you procrastinate when you feel angry toward your instructor or the nature of the course, *take a moment to focus on your long-term goals.* Remember why you are here and where you plan to go. Don't let emotional obstacles stand in your way. Make an appointment to calmly, politely, and rationally discuss your concerns with your instructor. Perhaps you can resolve the issue together. It will be good practice for life after college—in the workplace we are often required to foster a productive and civil working relationship with difficult people (more on that in Chapter 9).

STAYING OUT OF THE PITS

Let Me Count the Ways (Instead of Working)

Here is one student's "Top 10 List" for procrastinating:

1. I work best under time pressure so I'm going to wait and study later.
2. I'm too tired.
3. It's morning and I'm a night person—my body clock is out of sync.
4. My horoscope says it's a bad day for me.
5. It's too nice outside to be in here studying.
6. Study tonight? No way, my favorite TV shows are on.
7. This is going to give me a headache. I'm going to do something else.
8. Even if I do it, it probably won't be good enough, so why do it?
9. Ten years from now, will it really matter if I don't do this right now?
10. I think I'll wait until later when I become more motivated.

? Questions for Class Discussion

1. Are there too many demands on college students today in terms of time? If so, what are they?
2. Do you find yourself wasting time each day? If so, how?
3. What type of calendar do you prefer, paper or electronic? How did you make your choice?
4. What are your "big rocks"?
5. Why do people procrastinate? How is this harmful?
6. How can your family and friends help you to effectively manage your time?

Journal Assignment

Based on the "time diary" activity, consider how the way you spend your time currently fits with your life goals and priorities. To direct your writing, consider the following questions:

1. If someone who did not know me were to look at my time diary, what conclusions would he or she reach regarding my goals and priorities?
2. What new realizations did you reach as you completed the time diary activity?

3. Does your "ideal" weekly schedule differ from your current one? In what ways?

4. Will it be easy or difficult for you to stick to your ideal schedule? Why or why not?

Summary

- Effective time managers allocate daily, weekly, and monthly time according to established life goals and priorities.
- A "time diary" can help raise your level of self-awareness regarding the use of your time, whether or not your use of time fits with your goals, and can help you to identify pockets of wasted time.
- Top time wasters for college students include television, commuting, working too much, partying, and Internet use.
- Using a calendar, either paper or electronic, is critical for effective time management.
- Students should create monthly, weekly, and daily goals for every semester.
- Procrastination is habit-forming and can result in poor grades and increased stress.

Case Study

Natasha was a transfer student at Plains University. She was 30 years old, and a single mom with two daughters, ages six and ten. Natasha had attended college for one year out of high school, and then decided to marry and start a family. Her husband, Ned, was a successful businessman who provided well for his family. Natasha did not need to work outside of the home and greatly enjoyed the time she was able to spend with her children. She home schooled them, took them to swimming and horseback riding lessons, traveled in the summertime, and was quite happy with her life and the opportunities she was able to provide for the girls.

Then, while traveling on business, Ned was involved in a fatal automobile accident. Natasha was suddenly and tragically not only a single parent, but also a single parent without paid employment outside the home.

Natasha found herself needing to find a good job, but with limited education and no work experience Natasha had few opportunities for earning a living wage. She quickly realized she would need to return to college so that she could increase her employment opportunities and consequently her long-term earning potential. But Natasha also wanted to continue to home school her children, and provide for them as they were accustomed. Natasha did not want to go into debt—Ned's savvy business practices taught her that much—but how on earth would she be able to afford college and provide for her children?

Natasha was quite ambitious and decided that she could do it all. She would work the night shift at the convenience store down the street, take as many courses online as possible, bring her daughters to class with her in the mornings after work, and home school them in the late afternoon after her nap.

After about six weeks of this grueling schedule, Natasha felt exhausted, depressed, and frustrated. Her children were sad that they did not get to spend as much time with Mom, and when they did, she was tired and irritable. Natasha's academic performance was suffering as well.

🍴 Food for Thought

What are Natasha's "big rocks"? What changes might Natasha consider to help her achieve her academic goals?

Managing Your Money

6

> ["Money talks . . . but all mine ever says is good-bye."]
> — Anonymous

In a Student's Voice

"Oh, my situation is a little bit unusual. I am a nontraditional student, so maybe some of my answers are not going to be traditional, because some people take more classes a semester; they get a very high GPA, and they learn a lot; they join lots of activities and enjoy their experience on campus, and I think that is the right way to do it. I only take what I have to, to be full time. I am working two jobs; I don't have time for anything; I don't sleep; I don't eat. I'm overstressed all the time, but I'm going like—like the nonstop train."

—Virginia, transfer student
(Nowak, 2004)

Learning Objectives

- Understand the need for effective financial management
- Assess current income and expenditures
- Identify ways to minimize or eliminate excess spending
- Understand the advantages and risks of consumer credit
- Learn how to apply for federal financial aid
- Become aware of the various types and sources of financial aid

Quick Start Quiz

Assess your existing knowledge of key components of this chapter. Check each item below that applies to you:

- ❏   I can pinpoint where and how I spend my money.
- ❏   I have a plan for saving money.
- ❏   I have a detailed budget to guide my spending and saving.
- ❏   I use credit responsibly.
- ❏   I take steps to avoid being vulnerable to identify theft.

Is College Worth the Cost?

A college education is a significant financial investment, and the costs of college are on the rise. But your college education is one of the most worthwhile investments you'll ever make. College graduates can expect to earn much more than high school graduates every year of their professional lives. The National Center for Education Statistics (2006) reports that men who have earned a bachelor's degree or higher earn 67 percent more than men who have earned only a high school diploma. Over the course of a career, college graduates can expect to earn an average of more than $1,000,000 more than their peers with only a high school diploma. Your college diploma is definitely worth the four or five years you will spend sacrificing luxuries and living on a shoestring. But don't view your future earnings as license to spend foolishly and go into unnecessary debt. Poor money management skills may have a long-term impact on your credit rating, your employment prospects, and your long-term financial well being.

If you are living on your own for the first time, you may be managing your own money for the first time as well. Freedom to spend money as you choose is one of your newfound liberties as a college student at your new school, but it is also a very important responsibility. Just as skipping class and skimping on study time may do irreparable damage to your college transcript, spending foolishly or amassing debt may be devastating to your way of life and to your credit record.

Many college students find financial matters to be a source of distress. In a recent survey of college students in the state of New York, almost half—41 percent—reported that they felt "stressed and overwhelmed" about money. Only 42 percent of students reported that they had developed a personal budget, and only 15 percent could report exactly how they spent their money. At the same time, 26 percent of the students surveyed reported that they had paid at least $100 for a single pair of jeans in the past (Bank of America, 2005). These data suggest that college students should understand where their money is spent, develop a budget, and make financial decisions accordingly if they are to take control of their finances and avoid feeling stressed about money.

Bottom line: If you cannot find a financially responsible way to fund your education, you won't be able to complete your degree and maintain your fiscal health. Managing your money well is a key factor in your college success and will also build a foundation for sound financial practices in your future.

College tuition costs vary widely—please see the figure below for a comparison of tuition bills between different types of institutions.

Average academic year tuition and required fees for full-time students at Title IV institutions, by control of institution, and level of institution: United States, academic year 2004–05

Student level, level of institution, and first professional program	Public		Private	
	In-state	Out-of-state	Not-for-profit	For-profit
	Average tuition and required fees per institution			
Undergraduate				
4-year	$4,936	$12,088	$16,046	$13,063
2-year	2,412	5,332	8,182	11,248

Source: U.S. Census Bureau, Current Population Survey http://www.census.gov/
Internet Release Date: March 2005

How Do I Take Control of My Finances?

The first step toward becoming an effective money manager is to become precisely aware of all of your expenses, and all of your sources of income. Once you know exactly what you have and what you need, you will be able to create a budget for yourself or for your household. This budget will help you to live "within your means." In other words, a budget can help you to refrain from spending more than you earn. A budget also helps you make informed decisions about unplanned purchases or unexpected expenses. Creating and sticking to a budget is an excellent way to stay out of, or minimize, your debt.

Activity

In order to assess your daily and monthly expenses, it is helpful to keep a monthly "money diary" similar to the weekly "time diary" that you created in the previous chapter. Appendix D is a template that you can use to list your monthly expenses. Begin by including the fixed expenses that are easily identified: rent or mortgage or residence hall fee; car payment; insurance payment; and so on. If you do not pay some of these expenses monthly but rather semi-annually or at the end of each semester, then simply divide the cost by the number of months in the billing period to arrive at your monthly figure.

To fill in the amounts for your variable expenses, you'll need to carefully collect and retain receipts for incidental purchases that you make. For the purpose of this exercise, you may want to keep a tally of your incidental purchases for one week, and then multiply by four to estimate your monthly incidental expenses. The worksheet is simply a guideline; your expense categories may be somewhat different than those listed. Modify as needed. You may even prefer to re-create this worksheet as a spreadsheet on your computer; that way you can insert formulas for quick and accurate calculations.

The final section of the worksheet asks you to identify your income sources. These may include earned wages, scholarships, grants, or loans, family contributions, and so on. Write those down and add them up.

Once you have entered all of your monthly income and expenses, it is time to calculate the difference. Is your income greater than your expenses? If so, congratulations! You'll have money available for emergencies, so be sure to put it in a savings account where it will be safe and also earn interest for you. If your income is less than your expenses, you have work to do. You'll need to find ways to reduce your spending in order to live within your means, or consider ways you might increase your available income.

How Can I Stick to a Budget?

Using the information you collected in your monthly "money diary," you are now ready to create your monthly budget. If your expenses are greater than your income, carefully examine where your money is going. Just as we identified pockets of wasted time in the "time diary" exercise, can you identify instances of "wasted" money? Examples include dining out frequently; parking or traffic tickets; or little luxuries that may not be completely necessary, such as tickets to movies or sporting events. Most college students may need to make some sacrifices, or exchange pricey hobbies for inexpensive ones, in order to maintain financial health. As stated earlier, as a college graduate you will make more money over your lifetime than a noncollege graduate. Sound financial practices in college will certainly pay off in the long run.

Do you need to cut some of your costs? Here are a few ideas:

- Unless you have a prepaid meal plan on campus, consider bringing a lunch or light snacks with you to keep you from spending cash each day on food. Spending $5 to $8 daily for a meal can add up to $160 per month! Brown bagging will cost you a small fraction of that amount.
- Resist the urge to buy brand-new textbooks each semester. Most bookstores offer used books, or if not, you may be able to find used versions

of your required texts at competing bookstores in your community. Or you may be able to check out a copy of certain textbooks in your university library. Even if the books are on reserve and cannot be checked out, you can organize your study habits to allow for sufficient time to sit in the library and read, take notes, and photocopy from one or two required texts each semester.

- Look for student discounts in your community. Barber shops and beauty salons, dry cleaners, retailers, and other establishments frequently choose to attract student customers via discounts on products or services. The discounts may seem small but can add up over time.

- Buy in bulk. As you know, grocery outlets offer substantial savings when selling items in bulk. If you live alone or have little storage space, consider shopping with two or three friends, and then splitting the bulk purchases among the group.

- Minimize or eliminate car payments. Car payments can cut deeply into your monthly earnings, and they do not lower your income level for financial aid need assessment. Unlike mortgage payments on a home, car payments are not always a wise investment of money—cars depreciate rapidly in value. If you have hefty payments on an expensive car, consider selling it and either buying an inexpensive used car, or perhaps even a bicycle! You'll find that you will save a bundle of money on auto insurance as well.

- Going home for Thanksgiving or spring break? Shop around to find the best deals. There is no shortage of Internet travel sites to explore, including travelzoo.com, expedia.com, priceline.com, or orbitz.com. You can sign up to receive e-mail notifications of promotional fares or special deals.

- Don't gamble. Lottery tickets and the like are often dubbed "a tax for the mathematically challenged." Statistics indicate that it is extremely unlikely that you will make it rich by gambling, and that dollar or two spent on lotto tickets here and there can add up quickly. Some gamblers can even become addicted, thus creating an even more dangerous financial trap.

- Save money. Saving money each month may seem a Herculean task, especially if you've got a tight budget to begin with. But it is an excellent habit to cultivate, and it may even thwart a major financial snag should a major unexpected expense come along. Consider a monthly deposit into a savings account. Even a very small amount, such as $5, $10, or $20 a month, can add up over time, and it can collect interest as well.

- Finally, when needs arise that will cut deeply into your bank account, ask yourself if the purchase can wait. This may give you time to save some money toward the purchase, or it may give you an opportunity to drop a hint in the ear of a close friend or family member before your next birthday.

The Rising Cost of College

In the early days of American higher education, during the 18th century, college tuition plus room and board cost between $20 and $90 per year (Cohen, 1998).

Since then, costs have risen quite dramatically. The College Board reports that in 2005-2006, average yearly tuition costs for a four-year public school are $5,491, a seven percent increase over the previous year, and the average yearly tuition costs for a four-year private school are $21,235, a six percent increase over the 2004-2005 year. That's tuition alone, not including room, board, and textbooks.

Despite the price tag, a college education is a worthwhile investment. As mentioned above, over the course of a lifetime, a bachelor's degree can net you about $1,000,000 more than you would earn with only a high school diploma (College Board, 2005). So to maximize that differential, be sure to become a conscientious money manager!

Should I Use My Credit Cards in College?

If you're a college student, chances are, you have at least one credit card. If not, prepare to be courted by credit card companies wanting your business! You may see credit card company representatives on your campus, enticing you with free gifts, low initial interest rates, or reduced fees for signing up. But before you do, make sure you understand the fine print and have thought carefully about how you intend to use your credit card. Like so many things in life: food, computers, alcohol, or television—credit cards can be useful for a specific purpose, but can also be the source of much pain and misery if misused or abused.

Credit cards are useful for three things:

- Emergency situations that arise when you do not have cash on hand
- Establishing a good *credit history* by paying your balance in full, and on time, every month
- Tracking your monthly expenditures

Credit cards should not be used for these purposes:

- Spending money you do not have on items you could live without
- Elevating your social status
- Avoiding the reality of your temporary poverty as a college student

Americans love credit. And banks love the Americans who do! Did you know that more than $65 billion is paid to banks every year in credit card interest? That's because less than half of us in the United States pay our credit card balances in full every month (American Consumer Credit Counseling, 2005). If you do not pay your balance in full each month, the cost of credit can add up quickly. But if you make a pledge that you will pay your balance in full—thus living within your means—establishing a line of credit may be useful to you.

What's So Important About a Credit History?

After you graduate and have a steady job, you may want to consider purchasing a new home or automobile. Your credit history translates into your "credit score," a number that is what banks will use to determine how much of a credit "risk" you are. Your credit score is a number between 300 and 850, and it is calculated based solely on your credit history. A higher score indicates a lower credit risk. Lenders are restricted by law from considering race, gender, income, age, address, marital status, or employment history when evaluating your application for credit. Credit score distribution in the U.S. looks something like this:

  7 percent = 300–549
20 percent = 550–649
33 percent = 650–749
27 percent = 750–799
13 percent = over 800 (Holmes, 2005)

Lenders predict that consumers with high credit scores are more likely than not to repay their debts. If you've used your credit card wisely, and have paid off your balance in full each month for an extended period of time, then your credit rating will be a good one and you may qualify for the lowest interest rates available for your automobile loan or home mortgage. On the other hand, if you've made only the minimum payments on your credit card, or have been late with a payment or two, your credit rating will not be as good, and the opportunities for loans will be fewer, and with higher interest rates.

Consider this reality: although the best available interest rates will vary from month to month, in 2006 the average interest rate that Americans paid on a new car loan was between 6 and 7 percent. Consumers with poor credit can expect to pay between 19 and 26 percent interest, and enjoy a car payment that is up to *$200 per month higher* than the amounts that their colleagues with good credit will pay. If that's not painful enough, consumers with poor credit will also pay between 20 and 50 percent more on car insurance premiums than those with good credit (Sturgeon, 2005**).**

Sadly, riding your bicycle for a few years until your credit history improves will not solve all of your credit woes. About 70 percent of employers will check an applicant's credit history and use that information in the hiring decision. The rationale is that applicants with poor credit histories may be dealing with personal and/or legal problems that distract them from work, cause them to miss work, or cause collection agencies to call the office. Poor credit may also impact your ability to rent an apartment, have utilities connected, or purchase cellular telephone service contracts at a reasonable price (Sturgeon, 2005). You can see how going into more debt than you can afford ignites a downward spiral of increasing financial difficulties. A poor credit score creates an even steeper path toward financial health and stability.

To find out what your credit score is, you should contact each of the three major credit reporting companies:

Experian (www.experian.com)
TransUnion (www.transunion.com)
Equifax (www.equifax.com)

If your credit score is not as high as it should be, the best way to improve it is to consistently pay your bills on time, pay off debts, and check your credit report annually to be sure there are no inaccuracies. Mistakes can be made if loan payments are applied to the wrong account or social security numbers are entered incorrectly by your creditors. Don't apply for credit frequently—lenders interpret this as risky behavior, and it will lower your score. Keep up the good behavior and over time, the numbers will improve.

What Is the Real Cost of Credit?

Despite the horror stories, credit cards can be a useful resource if you clearly understand the fine print and use your card intelligently. Before you will be able to effectively evaluate a credit card offer, you will need to understand the terminology that banks use. Here are a few basic concepts:

- *Interest*: Amount charged for using the card, designated as a percentage.
- *APR*: Annual percentage rate. Expressed as a percentage, it helps you to compare offers.
- *Annual fee*: Fixed amount charged each year as long as your account is open.

- *Compounding interest*: An interest payment calculated on your daily, weekly, or monthly credit card balance. That amount is then added to the balance owed.
- *Principal*: The base amount charged, exclusive of accrued interest

As an example, suppose Big Bucks Bank (BBB) offers you a credit card at 18 percent interest, compounded monthly, with no annual fees, and a credit limit of $500. You choose to sign up for the card in September, and charge $500 worth of items the first month. The bill comes in October, and shows a minimum payment due of $10. This is about 2 percent of the balance, a minimum required by many banks. You send a check for $10 dutifully each month to Big Bucks Bank. You do not use your credit card again. By the following September, one year later, you've paid $120 toward your balance, but still owe $467.40! How can this be?

This is because at an 18 percent interest rate, compounded monthly, only $32.59 went toward the principal balance, and $87.41 accrued in interest. How long will it take to pay off your balance? If you do not add any charges to your account, and you pay only the minimum due each month, you will need an additional 84 months to pay off the remaining balance—nearly seven years. At the end of that time, you will have paid $431.08 in interest, raising the total cost of the original $500 purchase to $931.08. Ouch!

Some banks, however, are beginning to raise minimum payments from 2 percent to 4 percent. Bank of America, MBNA, and Citibank have made this change, and other major financial institutions are expected to do the same (Warnick, 2005). This can be either good or bad for the consumer, depending upon your perspective and your finances. The good news is that by paying more of your balance each month, you pay less in interest and pay off your debt sooner. The bad news is that if your budget is tight, it may become difficult to make the minimum payment. If you cannot make the minimum payment, you can damage your credit rating.

If you are expecting a lucrative job offer upon graduation, and feel you will be able to repay debts quickly, bear in mind that many of your living expenses will also rise—such as housing, clothing, and transportation—as you begin your professional career and desire to elevate your standard of living. You may even be starting a family at that point in your life. Reducing large credit card debts may take some time and dedication.

If you need any further convincing regarding the perils of credit card use, consider this: any credit card debt that you owe and payments that you are making do not improve your chances for receiving financial aid. Incurring credit card debt is considered to be a choice and not a necessity when your financial aid awards are being considered (Tanabe and Tanabe, 2004).

Identity Theft

Identify theft occurs when someone obtains your personal information, such as credit card number or social security number, and is then able to pretend to be you when making purchases or applying for credit. Even if you have little cash or assets, you can still be in danger, as identity thieves can obtain loans in your name, neglect to repay them, and thus quickly ruin your credit rating. The impact on your time and your finances can be substantial. Here are some tips for avoiding identity theft:

- Always keep your financial and personal information in a secure place. This includes credit cards, ATM or check cards, birth certificate, passport, and social security number. Never keep your PIN numbers in the same place as the cards to which they match. Keep a list of all of your bank account numbers and the corresponding telephone numbers in a separate location, so that you can cancel your accounts immediately should your wallet or handbag be stolen.

- Do not give out credit card or personal information over the telephone, or in response to e-mail inquires regarding your bank account. These inquiries may appear to come from reputable, recognizable financial institutions, but are usually fraudulent. If in doubt, contact the institution directly.

- Use good judgment when giving your credit card number or personal information on the Internet. Limit sending information only to trusted, well-known organizations. Make sure the Web page on which you enter your personal information is secure: check for "https" in the address rather than just "http"—the "s" stands for secure.

- If you need to discard receipts or other documents with personal or credit card information, shred them thoroughly before tossing them into the trash. You might consider purchasing a small personal shredder, especially if you receive credit card applications frequently in the mail. Identity thieves are known to rummage through garbage!

- Some colleges and universities still use social security numbers as student identification numbers. College staff and administrators understand the security issues involved and will most likely take great care to safeguard your information, but it is always a good idea to take charge of your own safety and security as much as possible. When asked to provide your full social security number on an assignment or form, ask if providing the last four digits will be sufficient.

- Open your bank and credit card statements immediately when they arrive in the mail or become available online. Review the information carefully, and report any unauthorized charges immediately.

- For further information, including what to do if you have become a victim of identity theft, visit the Federal Trade Commission's Web site: http://www.consumer.gov/idtheft/

What Kinds of Financial Aid Are Available?

Most students and their families cannot afford the entire cost of college on their own. The U.S. government, state governments, and countless private organizations help to make college affordable by allocating funds to assist college students. Each year, more than *80 billion dollars* in financial aid is awarded to students (Tanabe and Tanabe, 2004). That's a lot of cash! More than half of college undergraduates receive financial aid to help cover the cost of education (Wilkinson, 2005). You will want to make sure you know how much aid, and what types of aid, you are eligible to receive.

Financial aid comes in a wide variety of forms. Some must be repaid, and some is free money for you to keep. Although many students prefer not to go into debt in order to fund their education, a student loan may mean the difference between being able to continue your education and needing to stop out or drop out.

Some aid is awarded based on merit; some is awarded based on need; and some is awarded using a combination of various criteria. In this section, we'll discuss the types of aid available, how to apply, and matters to consider as you determine what type of aid to accept.

Types of Aid

1. *Grants.* These are some of the most attractive types of aid, because they do not need to be repaid. One of the largest grant programs is the Federal Pell Grant program. Pell Grants are for students with the greatest financial need and who have not yet earned a bachelor's degree. The maximum amount a student may receive per year was $4050 in 2006. In the 2003–2004 school year, 27 percent of undergraduates received Pell Grants. The average award for a full-time student was $3100 (National Center for Education Statistics, 2005).

2. *Scholarships.* Scholarships are similar to grants, in that they are free money awarded to you. Scholarships come from a wide variety of sources, and it will take some research on your part to identify those for which you qualify. Criteria for scholarships vary widely as well. Some are based on merit, e.g., ACT/SAT scores or college grade point average. Some are based on financial need. Many are for specific populations of students, such as physical science or humanities majors, or nontraditional female students. It may surprise you to know that some very savvy students can make money going to college by securing multiple scholarships and grants each year. These students make it part of their job to actively research funding opportunities, make applications religiously and frequently, and manage their "income sources" effectively. Don't

wait for money to come to you. It is out there, so go get it! Here are some places to begin your scholarship search:

- Your college or university financial aid office. Many schools have established scholarships for incoming students. Some have scholarships specifically for transfer students.
- Your academic department. If you are a philosophy major, for example, there may be an annual award for a student in your department.
- Professional associations for students in your academic discipline
- Student clubs or organizations
- Religious organizations
- Charities or local nonprofit groups
- Community service groups
- Your employer or your parents' employer(s)
- Websites: www.fastweb.com; www.collegeanswer.com; www.collegeboard.com; www.fedmoney.org. Your own Internet search may reveal many more possible search sites.

3. *Loans*. Unlike grants and scholarships, a student loan is an amount of money awarded to you that must be repaid in the future, with interest. The interest rates, however, are generally low in comparison with other types of consumer loans. The funds are loaned through the federal government or a bank. One federal program for students with exceptional financial need is the Perkins Loan. The interest rate is fixed at a very low 5 percent, and no interest accrues while you are enrolled in school. A nine-month grace period is extended to you after you leave school or graduate, before you must begin paying back your loan. Another federal program is the Stafford Loan. Stafford Loans carry a variable interest rate, not to exceed 8.25 percent. In 2003–2004, about 33 percent of undergraduates accepted Stafford Loans (National Center for Education Statistics, 2005). One important fact to remember about loan programs is that you must repay the loan, whether or not you ever complete your degree, and whether or not you were satisfied with your educational experience.

4. *Work Study*. The federal work study program awards aid in the form of wages earned for part-time work. The total award will vary based upon the student's need. Students who are eligible for work study may work on campus, or off campus in a public agency or nonprofit organization. Students will earn at least minimum wage, and sometimes higher, depending on the job. The employer pays 30 percent of the wage, and the federal government pays 70 percent of the wage. Students may work as many hours as they negotiate with the employer, up to the maximum amount of the work study award. Students are usually paid directly, via a check from the school. Eight percent of undergraduates received work study awards in 2003–2004

(National Center for Education Statistics, 2005). Work study is a good way to help finance your education, while building your resume as well.

Applying for Financial Aid

The first step toward receiving financial assistance for college is to complete the Free Application for Federal Student Aid (or FAFSA, for short). Note the word *free*—the form is free, and if you need assistance filling out the form, help is available for free as well. Beware of any person or organization that requires a fee to complete this form or give you assistance with the form—it's a scam. The FAFSA is required if you wish to be considered for any federal grant, loan, or work study award, and is often used at colleges and universities to evaluate students for internal aid programs.

You can complete the FAFSA online, at www.fafsa.edu.gov. That's the quickest way to get your form processed. If you prefer to fill in the form on paper, you may obtain a paper copy in your student financial aid office, the public library, or call 1-800-433-3243 and request a form to be mailed to you.

Time is of the essence when it comes to applying for aid. Although the FAFSA deadline is June 30 of each year for the school year beginning in August or September, many colleges and universities use FAFSA information to evaluate you for their internal financial aid programs. Those deadlines may be much earlier in the year. Contact your school financial aid office for information. You can fill out your FAFSA as early as January 1 of each year, as long as you have your tax information available (W-2 forms, tax return form). You will need your parents' tax information if you are a dependent.

After your FAFSA has been processed, you will receive a Student Aid Report in the mail. The Student Aid Report contains your Expected Family Contribution figure. This is the amount of money that the government has calculated that you (or your family, if you are a dependent) can reasonably be expected to contribute to your college education each year. The difference between the cost of your college and your expected family contribution will be your financial need, or the amount of aid you may be eligible to receive. You may or may not be awarded sufficient aid to cover all of your need.

On Your Campus

This week, find out where your financial aid office is located. Visit with a financial counselor to discuss all of your options for paying for school. You should determine what college scholarship programs you may be eligible for. Ask about local community organizations that also offer college scholarships. Pick up as many applications as possible, and note the application deadlines.

Repaying Loans

The terms of repayment vary by the type of loan that you have. One thing that they have in common, however, is the fact that they *must be repaid*. Generally, the only conditions under which loans will be forgiven are if the student suffers (a) a permanent and complete disability, or (b) death. If you neglect to make payments on your loan, after a specified period of time you will be in *default* status. When you enter default status, the following negative consequences will ensue:

- Credit bureaus will be notified, and your credit rating will suffer
- Your income tax refund may be withheld and applied to the balance owed
- You will not be eligible for federal aid, should you decide to continue your education

However, loan programs offer some flexibility to help you avoid default status, should you have trouble finding a job immediately upon graduation, or suffer other financial difficulties. Federal loan programs offer the student a grace period after leaving school, graduating, or falling below half-time enrollment status. The Perkins Loan offers a nine-month grace period. Stafford loans offer a six-month grace period. You may or may not accrue interest charges on the unpaid balance during the grace period, depending on whether or not your loan was subsidized by the government.

You also have a long time to repay the loan. A Perkins Loan must be repaid in 10 years. A Stafford Loan may be repaid anywhere from 10 to 30 years. Stafford loan programs also offer you the opportunity to vary your loan payments—start out low, and increase gradually, or base the loan payment amount on the salary that you are earning.

If you have trouble making your payments, you may qualify for *deferment* or *forbearance*. You may be able to defer your loan payments for up to three years due to underemployment or unemployment, or economic hardship for other reasons. The interest may or may not accrue during this time, depending upon the type of loan you have. If you do not qualify for a deferment, you may be eligible for a forbearance of up to one year. Interest will accrue while you are in forbearance status.

For further detail regarding federal loan repayment, visit this Web site: www.studentaid.ed.gov/pubs.

In summary, taking out loans should be considered carefully. Be sure you understand the terms of your loan before you sign on the dotted line. You may be paying on the loan for many years to come. However, most student loans carry a lower interest rate than other types of loans, and are likely a better alternative than ending or interrupting your college education.

Tax Breaks

At the time of this writing, two federal programs were available that may help reduce the amount of tax that you owe each year based on your educational expenses.

The Hope tax credit can reduce the federal income tax that you owe based on the money you have spent on tuition for the previous tax year, up to $1500. First- and second-year college students may qualify. One hundred percent of the first 1000 tuition dollars that you have spent and 50 percent of the second $1000 may be claimed. This amount must be tuition dollars spent out of your pocket, not paid for via scholarships or grants. Your annual income will impact the amount for which you qualify.

The Lifetime Learning Credit is for both undergraduate and graduate students in any year of their degree programs. You can calculate the tax credit that you may receive by taking 20 percent of the tuition that you have paid, up to $10,000. This amount must also be tuition dollars spent out of your pocket, not paid for via scholarships or grants. The maximum tax credit is $2000. The forms that you will use vary depending upon your income and other tax deductions you may have. Tax laws are subject to change. For more information, visit your local tax professional, or visit http://www.irs.gov.

I'm Married—How Can We Agree on Money Matters?

Financial matters can be one of the most divisive issues for couples. If unresolved, financial stress can result in separation or divorce. Personal preferences, lifestyle goals, values, locus of control, and lifelong habits all impact our attitudes and behaviors toward money. Couples may wed with certain expectations regarding money management. They may also have entered into the marriage with varying levels of personal debt. When attitudes or behaviors toward money come into conflict, marital bliss can dissolve into marital blues. But there is hope!

Open and ongoing communication is the most important first step toward a mutually agreeable financial plan. Set aside some time, send the children to the neighbor's house, turn off the television, and focus on your finances for an hour or two. If you've done the budget exercise earlier in this chapter, then you have a starting point for discussion. Identify and agree upon your short- and long-term financial goals, and determine if your current pattern of saving, spending, and debt management is consistent with your goals. Consider your current and future lifestyle preferences. Can they become a reality given your current financial behavior? If not, what changes can you agree to make?

If record keeping is a divisive issue for the two of you, a second matter to consider is whether or not separate accounts or a combined account is the best approach. A joint checking account can create trouble spots for couples with differing approaches to record keeping. If he diligently enters each check or check card transaction and then calculates the remaining balance, while she prefers to keep a week's worth of receipts in her purse before entering them in the register, trouble may be brewing. If both parties are writing checks or using their check cards without daily reconciliation, the account may become overdrawn or an electronic transaction denied. One solution may be to put the more detail-oriented partner in charge of the checkbook. He or she will maintain the register, serve as the keeper of check card receipts, and will reconcile the statement promptly each month.

Another solution may be to create two separate accounts. This solution allows each party to manage money as he or she chooses. It may also protect cash assets in the event that you split up and one partner has contributed much more to the account than the other—in community property states a joint account will be divided equally. Separate accounts are also a good idea if you're sharing finances but not yet married—you won't have additional squabbles regarding money should the relationship sour.

Bottom line: Talk to each other. Acknowledge your differences, and come to an agreement regarding your financial goals and daily strategies for getting there. When money matters are no longer a major source of frustration, you'll find it much easier to maintain a healthy and happy relationship.

? Questions for Class Discussion

1. What are some of the reasons students find it difficult to stick to a budget?
2. What are some of the ways you might spend money unnecessarily?
3. What tips can you share with your classmates for cutting costs in your daily routine?
4. Do Americans use credit too much? Why or why not?
5. Should college students have credit cards? Why or why not?
6. Who is to blame when people incur debt they cannot repay—themselves or the credit card companies?

Journal Assignment

In your journal this week, reflect on what money means to you. Write one to two pages. To direct your writing, consider these questions:

1. Do you enjoy spending money, or do you prefer to save it? Why do you believe this is so?

2. Imagine that it is now five years after you graduated from college. You have the job of your dreams, and the lifestyle you've always wanted. Describe in detail what a typical day is like for you.

3. With the scenario in item #2 in mind, how much money will you need to have to achieve your goals? Is this realistic given your current money management style?

4. Do you stress out over money? Describe some of the feelings that you experience when you attend to your finances.

Summary

- College students must become effective money managers in order to finance their education and minimize financial stress.
- Assessing income and expenses and creating a budget are the first steps toward taking control of finances.
- Students must understand the advantages and risks of consumer credit cards before deciding to accept one.
- Financial aid comes in many forms and from various sources.
- Students should investigate all possible options for aid in order to maximize financial assistance.
- Students should understand the terms and conditions for loan repayment before taking out loans.

Case Study

Taylor grew up in a very rural area of her state. Her family had owned a small farm for several generations. Taylor's parents had not attended college, and made a very modest living on the farm. However, the farm was not likely to be viable for much longer, and Taylor and her family knew that she must earn a college degree in order to expand her career opportunities.

Taylor graduated at the top of her high school class, and scored extremely well on the ACT exam. She easily met the admissions standards for the large state universities but felt intimidated by the size of the campuses. Her community and high school were quite small, so Taylor opted to attend a nearby community college for the first year where the classes would be smaller and where she would know some of the students.

At the end of her first year, Taylor had earned perfect grades and landed a full scholarship to Concordia, a prestigious private university several hours away from home. She was both excited and apprehensive as she made the transition to a whole new world.

Although Taylor's tuition would be waived, she would need additional aid toward her living expenses. Taylor completed the FAFSA and learned that she was eligible for work study and a Pell Grant. She knew that in addition to the financial aid, she would need to find ways to minimize her expenses as well. Taylor combed the local newspaper for other students seeking roommates, and quickly found a reasonable room in a small apartment with another second-year student. Taylor's apartment was about a half mile from campus, so she was able to depend on her bicycle to get to school and back. She took public transportation when she needed to travel a greater distance. Taylor found a good part-time work study job on campus, and her monthly paycheck was enough to cover her rent, leaving the grant money to cover groceries and utilities.

As the semester progressed, Taylor could not help but notice that she dressed quite differently from the other female students at Concordia. Growing up in her rural community, Taylor always wore blue jeans and t-shirts, and owned only a simple pair of sneakers and well-worn cowboy boots in comparison to her roommate's closet full of pumps, sandals, and spike-heeled boots. Taylor decided to invest in a new wardrobe. She did not have nearly enough money to buy the brands of clothing and accessories that she wanted, so she decided to apply for a credit card. After all, she reasoned, she might need it for emergencies.

As soon as the new card arrived, Taylor and her roommate spent a day at the local shopping mall, and easily charged $1000 in clothes, shoes, and makeup. Taylor's self-confidence blossomed in her new image, and she found herself meeting new people much more easily. Her social life took off! Taylor's new friends invited her on a long weekend road trip to the beach. Taylor desperately wanted to go, so she again pulled out her credit card.

By the end of the fall semester, Taylor found herself in $2500 of credit card debt. The minimum payments were $50. This was not a lot to her new friends, but more than Taylor could now afford to pay. Her parents were not in a position to help out, and Taylor was already working as much as her work study award would allow. She became stressed and depressed, and began to consider dropping out of school until she could pay off her credit card balance.

¶¶/ Food for Thought

In what other ways could Taylor achieve her social goals without going into debt? What strategies might she follow now to get out of debt?

Staying Well

$$\left[\begin{array}{l}\text{"Good health and good sense are two of life's}\\ \text{greatest blessings."}\\ \hspace{3cm}\text{—Publius Syrus (42 BC)}\end{array}\right]$$

In a Student's Voice

"I definitely advise students to use the services more than I did. I've always just been like really independent minded and really didn't want to ask for help from anyone. I think if I had used the services that were here, you know gone to more of the orientation things and really just sort of become more involved right at the start, I think I would feel . . . Because I don't feel particularly at home here necessarily. I mean in the school. I mean this area's where I live but I don't feel particularly, like much of an attachment. Whereas I think a lot of other people do feel more of an attachment and that's because they stepped outside their comfort zone and asked for help or made an effort to take the time to do things."

—Andrew, transfer student
(Nowak, 2004)

Learning Objectives

- Understand the relationship between physical health and college success
- Become aware of the role of exercise in overall health
- Learn basic principles of proper nutrition
- Understand the risks associated with substance abuse
- Learn how to manage stress
- Understand the importance of adequate sleep
- Become aware of the importance of good mental health

Quick Start Quiz

Assess your existing knowledge of key components of this chapter. Check each item below that applies to you:

- ❑ I can describe elements of the five basic food groups.
- ❑ I understand the risks and benefits of energy drinks.
- ❑ If I use alcohol, I have a strategy for drinking responsibly.
- ❑ I have a plan for managing my stress.
- ❑ I make time for adequate sleep each night.

What Is the Connection Between Academics and Physical Health?

Did you ever do poorly on an exam or assignment because you did not feel well, were feeling sad, or were overtired? If so, you know from experience that human beings cannot perform at an optimum level when they are not feeling physically or mentally at their best. How we feel mentally and physically at any given moment is largely within our personal control. We all make choices every day that directly impact our health and overall sense of well being. The type of food that you eat, whether or not you exercise, the amount of caffeine or alcohol that you use, and even the amount of sleep that you get at night are daily choices that can enhance—or sabotage—your success in college. In this chapter you will learn what types of habits will lead to overall physical and mental health, and you will learn to identify those habits or behaviors that currently may be inconsistent with your academic and personal goals.

Do I Have to Exercise?

Our ancestors in ancient times did not have to worry much about exercise. The necessary survival tasks including hunting for food, maintaining shelter, raising crops, and preparing food kept their bodies moving throughout the day. Today, we are both blessed and cursed by modern conveniences. We can ride in a car to get to wherever we need to go, we may work or study seated at a desk most of the day, and we can microwave a packaged meal when we get hungry. Given our modern conveniences and the nature of work or school life, it is very easy to become inactive. The consequences of a sedentary lifestyle include obesity, heart disease, high cholesterol, diabetes, and other serious health risks. Exercise needs to be a daily priority in order to minimize these risks and help you stay healthy and feeling good.

Daily exercise has many benefits. It helps build strong bones. It can lower cholesterol levels. It can help you to increase your lean muscle mass, thus helping you to look trimmer. Muscle weighs more than fat, so a fit person may weigh the same as a chubby person, but wear a smaller size. Knowing you look great in your clothes can help to improve your self-image, self-esteem, and self-confidence. Exercise helps reduce stress and anxiety, and can help you to sleep better, too. With all of these benefits, what are you waiting for?

Thirty minutes of aerobic exercise each day can help keep you healthy. Exercise for longer periods of time to help improve your fitness level. Many college campuses have a student recreation center where students can lift weights, jog, swim, or use exercise machines. Making a visit to the recreation center a regular daily habit is a great idea. If you lack the self-discipline to consistently visit the center on your own, you might consider registering for an exercise class. Many colleges offer aerobics, tennis and racquetball, jogging, or swimming classes that you can enroll in for credit. You know you can't skip class lest you fail the course! Or find a friend with whom to work out every day. Something as simple as a brisk walk in the mornings will be very beneficial to both of you. You'll be able to "multitask" by integrating your social life and your workout routine! Establishing exercise as a regular habit as a young person will help you to maintain that habit throughout your lifetime. If you're not especially young now, it is never too late to begin. Regular exercise will help you to live a longer, happier, and more productive life.

How Do I Choose Healthy Foods?

Proper nutrition is critical for your long-term health, happiness, and vitality. What is proper nutrition? In *Dietary Guidelines for Americans 2005*, the U.S. Department of Agriculture outlined the most recent recommendations for a proper diet. A proper diet includes foods from the five basic food groups: meats and beans, milk, fruits, vegetables, and grains. Here is a summary of the key recommendations:

- Choose foods from the five basic food groups that have high levels of nutrients.
- Avoid foods high in saturated or trans fats, sugar, salt, and alcohol.
- Limit calories to those needed for a healthy weight given your age, gender, and level of physical activity.

The "meats and beans" food group includes familiar cuts of meat such as beef, chicken, pork, lamb, fish, and others. The USDA recommends choosing lean cuts of any type of meat that you eat. This group also includes beans, such as black beans, kidney beans, lima beans, lentils, and others due to their high protein content.

The "milk" category includes milk, cheese, and yogurt. These foods are high in calcium. Again, the USDA recommends sticking to low fat or nonfat choices within this group. If you cannot tolerate milk, you may find lactose-free products available in the grocery store. The USDA recommends three cups of foods from this group daily, for both men and women.

The "fruits" group includes all fruits and fruit juices. Fruit can be canned, frozen, or fresh. Choose fresh fruit when possible to offer you the highest nutritional value for your calorie dollar. Fruit juices offer the same nutritional value as fresh fruit, but lack the bulk and fiber. For example, one medium fresh orange contains about 70 calories, while eight ounces of orange juice contain about 110 calories. Both offer more than enough vitamin C for the day, but the fresh orange will also provide you with about three grams of fiber and may help your tummy to feel fuller.

The "vegetables" group includes a vast array of foods offering a broad variety of nutritional values. The USDA has created five subgroups based on the primary nutrients that each vegetable contains. The "dark green" group includes foods such as spinach, kale, and broccoli. The "orange" group includes carrots, pumpkin, and sweet potatoes. The "starch" group includes corn, peas, and potatoes. Dry beans and peas and "other" make up the final two groups.

The final group, "grains," is subdivided into two categories, "whole grains" and "refined grains." Whole grains are foods such as oatmeal, whole wheat bread, or brown rice. Refined grains include white bread, white rice, and spaghetti. The refining process removes many of the nutrients of whole grains, as well as fiber, but some companies put those nutrients back in, a process known as "enriching." The enrichment process, however, cannot replace the fiber that has been removed (USDA, 2005).

If you find it difficult to stick to a balanced and nutritious diet each day on your own, consider purchasing a campus pre-paid meal plan. Studies have shown that students with meal plans generally eat healthier than students who shop and cook on their own (Brown, 2005). It makes sense—your campus dining hall staff will do the shopping for you, as well as wash, chop, and bake, thus saving you time while offering a variety of healthy choices every day. And they will do the dishes for you, too! Resist the temptation, however, to overeat if your meal plan includes "all you can eat" dining options. Small excesses here and there may add up quickly to unwanted pounds.

Can I Stick to a Vegetarian Diet?

Many people choose a vegetarian diet for health reasons, as animal products can be high in fat and cholesterol. Others choose to become vegetarian for social and environmental reasons: some contend that if the agricultural land used to raise cattle were used to produce grain instead, more mouths on our planet could be fed. And still others boycott animal products on the premise that raising animals for slaughter is cruel and inhumane. Whatever the reason, if you choose to eat "low on the food chain," you will need to make sure your diet is nutritionally sound.

There are three levels of vegetarian diets, ranging from very rigid to quite flexible. The more rigid the diet, the more nutrients may be excluded.

- Vegan—the vegan diet is the most restrictive. Vegans generally neither consume nor use any animal products whatsoever. If you are a vegan, you will exclude all meat, poultry, seafood, dairy products such as eggs, milk, and cheese, and even honey from your diet. Some vegans also reject use of animal products for any purpose, and will not purchase or wear shoes or clothing made of leather.
- Lacto vegetarian—this person will exclude meat, poultry, eggs, and seafood, but will consume milk, yogurt, and cheese.
- Lacto-ovo vegetarian—the lacto-ovo diet is similar to the lacto diet, but will include the consumption of eggs.

The more foods you exclude from your diet, the more vulnerable you become to deficiencies in necessary protein, vitamins, and minerals. It will be important to assess the amount of protein that you need to maintain a healthy body weight, and to ensure that you are consuming enough protein each day. About .36 grams of protein are needed per pound to maintain a certain body weight (USDA, 2005). So for example, if you weigh 125 pounds, you would need 45 grams of protein per day; if you weigh 150 pounds, you would need 54 grams per day to maintain your weight, and so on. Although animal products are typically denser in protein than plant products, with some careful planning it is not difficult for any vegetarian to meet recommended dietary protein needs.

For example, a 150-pound vegan can easily consume 54 grams of protein during an average day, as follows:

Breakfast:	Bagel with two tablespoons of peanut butter:	18 grams protein
Lunch:	Veggie burger	8 grams protein
Dinner:	One mug of black bean soup including one-half cup tofu:	28 grams protein
Total:		54 grams protein

Other sources of plant protein include pasta, rice, lentils, and chickpeas. Check food packaging of any product to determine protein content per serving.

Vegetarian diets, particularly vegan diets, may be deficient in minerals such as calcium, iron, and zinc. These three minerals are typically found in animal products but not in all plant products. Lacto and lacto-ovo vegetarians can easily consume sufficient calcium via dairy products. Vegans should include green leafy vegetables each day to provide calcium. Some examples are broccoli, bok choy, and kale. Iron and zinc can be found in fortified breakfast cereals, or dried beans and seeds.

Are Energy Drinks Good for Me?

Power bars, sports drinks, and energy drinks promise quick nutrition and fatigue relief. But are energy bars and drinks really a good idea? They can be, if your lifestyle is quite active and busy, and you sometimes need a quick pre-workout pick-me-up, or you occasionally lack time for a sit-down meal. But a power bar or sports drink is no more nutritious than a container of yogurt or a banana. What they offer is convenience—throw a couple of power bars in your backpack and you've got a reasonably healthy snack at the ready when your schedule is packed to the brim. The danger is eating these types of foods in addition to everything you would normally eat; at that point you are simply downing unnecessary calories.

Energy drinks can be harmful, however, when mixed with alcohol. Many young adults feel that combining vodka, whisky, or other spirits with an energy drink such as Red Bull will allow them to party longer and increase the stimulant effect of the alcohol. A recent study, however, dispels this notion: After subjects consumed either an energy drink, plain water, alcohol, or alcohol plus an energy drink, tests revealed no significant differences in performance or mood-boosting effects (Ferreria et al., 2004). More importantly, however, mixing a stimulant such as an energy drink with a depressant, such as alcohol, can cause health problems. Large doses of caffeine are problematic for anyone with conditions such as high blood pressure or anxiety. On top of that, large doses of caffeine can mask the effects of alcohol, thus rendering one unaware of the amount of alcohol consumed (Peck, 2001). Too much alcohol at one time can lead to alcohol poisoning, or even death. More on this matter in the next section.

What About Partying?

Alcohol is by far the most abused substance on college campuses. Indeed, for millions of college students, the use of alcohol seems to be deeply woven into the fabric of college life. Weekend parties, dates, football games, and other social events often revolve around the presence of alcohol. Alcohol use does not necessarily result in negative consequences, if used intelligently and in moderation. But for many students, drinking means drinking to get drunk, and the consequences can include reckless behavior, injury, and even death.

The most dangerous type of drinking behavior is called heavy or binge drinking. Heavy or binge drinking is defined as five or more drinks in a row for men, and four or more drinks in a row for women. This behavior can result in any number of tragic consequences. Hingson et al. (2005) report that about one in every five college students engages in binge drinking. The study also found that alcohol-related deaths among college students are on the rise, reporting an increase from 1600 in 1998 to 1700 in 2001. Death can result from injury or accident, or alcohol poisoning. About 2.8 million college students reported driving an automobile under the influence in 2001, up from 2.3 million in 1998. The study also discovered that more than 500,000 college students were injured during both years while under the influence, and 600,000 were assaulted by another student who had been drinking.

So the message is clear: heavy drinking puts you, and those around you, at risk for bodily injury. But there are other, more common effects from drinking. A recent survey, conducted with more than 68,000 college students, found that many of them suffered unpleasant consequences due to drinking. More than sixty percent reported having a hangover at least once, and more than half of the students reported feeling ill or vomiting after alcohol use. Thirty-nine percent later regretted some type of behavior that they engaged in while drinking. Thirty percent reported driving under the influence, and 33 percent missed one or more classes after a night of drinking. Finally, students who drink to excess are far more likely to engage in risky sexual behavior, or to have sex with someone they would not have had sex with had they been sober (Core Institute, 2004).

Since staying up late while drinking, and consequently waking up late or generally feeling lousy the next morning is a common result of heavy alcohol use, missing class is common for college student drinkers. And as you know, regular class attendance is one of the most important strategies for academic success. Therefore it should not surprise you to learn that the more you drink, the lower your grades will probably become. The CORE survey revealed an interesting— and expected—correlation between drinking behavior and grade point average. Of students who chose to use alcohol, students with an "A" average consumed 3.6 drinks per week; students with a "B" average consumed 5.5 drinks per week; "C" average students drank about 7.6 drinks each week, and finally those with a "D" average tallied 10.6 drinks per week.

Alcohol also contains calories, while delivering virtually no nutritional benefits. One 12-ounce can of regular beer has about 150 calories; light beer about 95. A five-ounce glass of white table wine has about 100 calories. One jigger of 80-proof rum, vodka, gin, or whisky has 94 calories. Multiplied by several times throughout the course of an evening, these empty calories can add significantly to your daily calorie total. Blender drinks contain a lot of sugar, and are particularly fattening. For example, a 6.8-ounce canned pina colada drink contains 526 calories! It is not difficult to see how drinking alcohol frequently or heavily may pack on unwanted pounds in a hurry.

So does this mean students should not drink at all? For some college students—about 20 percent—steering clear of alcohol altogether works well. And tee-totaling does not mean eliminating your social life—students who choose not to drink can still go to parties and have a good time, or attend events that do not revolve around alcohol. The remaining 80 percent of you, however, will need to be sure to follow the rules of responsible alcohol use if you want to minimize or eliminate the negative consequences of alcohol use in your life.

How Much Is "Just One"?

Moderate and responsible drinking behavior begins with an understanding of how much alcohol is in "one" drink. One drink is 1.25 ounces of 80 proof liquor, 12 ounces of beer, or 5 ounces of wine. How do you tell how much you are drinking when all of the drinks served at the keg party come in a big plastic cup? A sixteen-ounce plastic cup, filled to the top with beer, would be 1.3 drinks. If filled with wine, it equals 3.2 drinks. Monitor your intake closely while you are drinking, and if consuming mixed drinks, mix your own to be sure you know how much alcohol you are really consuming. Soda and juice can easily disguise the taste of hard alcohol in a strong drink, and leave you unintentionally drunk very quickly.

It is very possible to maximize the good effects of alcohol at a party and minimize the negative effects. Andreatta (2006) offers a strategy to help you achieve this goal. If you drink, you already know that the good feeling associated with alcohol—known as "the buzz"—happens relatively quickly when you begin to drink. As your blood alcohol content rises, you begin to feel relaxed, maybe a little less shy or inhibited, and a little more talkative. These good feelings will predominate as you continue to drink, up to a blood alcohol level of .055 percent. This is about two drinks in an hour for a 150-pound-man, and about one drink for a 100-pound-woman. This level is also your target level for the evening if you want to enjoy alcohol with minimal negative effects. Keep in mind that when it comes to alcohol, a little may be benign; more can be dangerous. You do not want to raise your blood alcohol level beyond .055. Beyond .055, up to about .08 blood alcohol content, speech, vision, motor skills, and judgment become impaired. This is also the level that many states determine to be above the legal limit for operating an automobile. At .10 percent, some people become loud and aggressive, and may not be able to recall how much they have had to drink. At this point and beyond you are at risk to yourself and others. So, if you choose to drink at a party, your strategy is to keep your blood alcohol level no higher than .055 for the duration of the party, and let it diminish about an hour or so before you depart for home. Here are some tips to help you maintain your goal:

- Arrange for a designated driver who will not drink at all to provide transportation to and from the party. It is generally a bad idea to operate an automobile with any amount of alcohol in your system.
- Always eat a reasonable meal before the party. Food will help slow the absorption of alcohol.
- Decide in advance how much you intend to drink, and during the party keep track of how many drinks you have had. After you begin drinking, your judgment about how much is too much for you will become cloudy. Stick to your predetermined limit.
- Drink slowly; never gulp.
- Pay attention to how you feel after one or two drinks—where your blood alcohol level is likely to be in the target zone.
- Try to adjust your intake to maintain the "buzz" without going above this level and becoming intoxicated. Alternating alcoholic beverages with nonalcoholic beverages is a good way to help keep your blood alcohol in the target zone.
- Don't play drinking games or guzzle alcohol, or encourage others to do so.
- Don't associate with people who drink heavily and pressure others to do so as well.
- Finally, drink a tall glass of water upon your return home to restore your hydration level.

Follow these guidelines for a safe, happy social outing and a happy, healthy morning after!

On Your Campus

This week, explore campus social activities that do not involve alcohol. Consult the student newspaper, bulletin boards, and campus organizations to find at least three events you would be interested in attending. Then, mark your calendar and bring a friend!

But Caffeine Is a Good Thing, Right?

Caffeine, like alcohol, can have desirable effects when used in moderation, and can have negative effects when abused. Caffeine can help us to concentrate, stay alert, and become energized. Too much caffeine, however, makes us jittery, irritable, and can interfere with sleep. Caffeine is also a diuretic. Too much can cause you to become dehydrated.

If you have high blood pressure, or suffer from chronic anxiety, you should be aware of the foods that contain caffeine, and make an effort to avoid them. Caffeine will only worsen your symptoms. Caffeine is found in coffee, of course, and energy drinks such as Red Bull, but is also found (albeit in lower levels) in soft drinks, tea, and chocolate.

Many students abuse caffeine in order to stay awake so that they can finish assignments, study late at night, or even engage in late-night computer gaming sessions. This is never a good idea for health reasons and academic ones. You'll remember from the chapters on study skills that proper planning and prioritizing should eliminate the need to pull "all-nighters" and will help to maintain your overall mental and physical health.

If you have been consuming a lot of caffeine for an extended time, decrease your use gradually. Going "cold turkey" may result in headaches or drowsiness. You may want to mix decaf coffee with regular coffee in the mornings, or even substitute tea for a few weeks. If you are a soda drinker, try caffeine-free versions of your favorite brand. Drinking lots of water is always a good idea as well.

What About Smoking?

The wash of negative publicity that nicotine has received in recent years virtually guarantees that everyone knows tobacco is bad for you. Very serious consequences such as emphysema and lung cancer can be the result of years of smoking. Yet, many people continue to smoke despite the dire health warnings. Why? Nicotine is extremely addictive. Once you're hooked, it is very hard to quit.

If you are not a smoker, and have never been, chances are by this point in your life becoming addicted to nicotine is not likely. If, however, the *stress* of your new school and obligations is prompting you to seek a chemical fix, by all means avoid cigarettes. Physical exercise, meditation, talking with a close friend, or even journaling are all wonderfully healthy ways to ease your stress without chemicals.

If you do smoke and need to quit, consider many of the cessation products on the market. When you consider the amount of money you are currently spending on your nicotine habit, as well as the investment you are making in your health, these products may not be as costly as they seem. Be prepared, however, when cravings occur. Many former smokers carry sugar-free breath mints or chewing gum to help satisfy the oral cravings without adding calories throughout the day. Be prepared as well to overcome the loss of your daily habits and rituals that had been centered around smoking. Stress balls, rubber bands, or a doodle pad may give your hands something to do when you are in situations in which you used to smoke. You may find that you will need to limit your association with your friends who smoke until the cravings subside.

Finally, be prepared for a probable weight gain. Nicotine increases your body's metabolic rate, which means you have been burning more calories as a smoker. In addition, the food you eat will begin to taste better after you quit, because the sensitivity of taste buds is decreased by nicotine and recovers once you stop smoking. A slightly lower metabolism, coupled with food that is more appealing to your tongue will probably add up to five or ten pounds. So if you're getting ready to quit, read the section on exercise once more—now is a great time to begin!

The bottom line on smoking is that no amount is safe or recommended. Steer clear of nicotine and encourage others to do the same.

The Cost of Smoking

1/2 PACK-A-DAY SMOKER

$5.00/pack × 3.5 packs/week = $17.50/week
$17.50/week × 52 weeks/year = $910.00/year
$910/year × 4 years of college = $3,640.00

In 25 years you will have spent $22,750 on cigarettes.

PACK-A-DAY SMOKER

$5.00/pack × 7 packs/week = $35.00/week
$35.00/week × 52 weeks/year = $1,820.00/year
$1,820/year × 4 years of college = $7,280.00

In 25 years you will have spent $45,500 on cigarettes.

I'm Stressed—What Can I Do?

Let's face it: stress is, and will always be, part of our daily lives. You might be reflecting on just the stress you've lived through so far today: perhaps a child woke up sick, or you were late for class or for work, or maybe you had an argument with your roommate or spouse. Little things can add up over the course of a day or a week, and leave us feeling "stressed out." And feeling overwhelmed by stress will undoubtedly make you irritable, depressed, anxious, and sometimes even physically ill. There is no way to avoid stress altogether, so in this section we'll discuss ways to manage your stress level and maintain your sanity.

Change, even when for the better, is naturally stressful. Your situation as a new transfer student is bound to produce many new stressors. You may be living in a new house or apartment, you may be in a new city or town, and perhaps you are now living with people whom you have just met. You may be faced with more financial challenges. You may be making major decisions regarding your academic plans and intended career path. All of these types of things can be very stressful for students.

Not all stress is "bad" stress, however. Stress can be viewed as a continuum, with no stress at one end and extreme stress on the other. Indeed, we all need a little bit of stress to keep us alert and engaged in daily activities. For example, experiencing just a little bit of anxiety before an exam is perfectly normal and actually helpful. The anxiety-invoked adrenaline that is pumping through your veins will help you to stay alert and focused on your task. Alternatively, if you are not anxious at all during the exam and are instead feeling extremely relaxed or sleepy, you may not give the exam your full attention. Or, on the other end of the continuum, very high levels of anxiety may inhibit recall of the material that you had studied during the preceding weeks and days. We could apply the same principle to driving a car during bad weather or getting ready to swing a golf club during a particularly difficult match. A little stress helps you perform at your best, but too much can be counterproductive.

When does a little bit of "good" stress balloon into "bad" stress? This varies greatly between people, and between situations. The level of stress that we feel is actually an individual reaction to the circumstances of the moment. You have probably noticed that certain situations stress some people out, but not others. For example, you may be able to navigate your way through big-city rush hour traffic with little stress, or calmly clean a child's bloody wound after a bad fall from a bicycle, but the same situations might feel overwhelming for your roommate. There may, however, be days when these situations *do* stress *you* out—for example, if the drive through big-city traffic occurs just after your wallet has been stolen or you lost your job. The stress builds up, and at some point you find yourself unable to cope with everyday situations.

People react differently to stress. Some experience physical sensations, such as sweaty palms, upset stomach, headaches, or fatigue. Some experience an emotional response, such as irritability, feeling frightened or anxious, or frequent mood swings. Still others respond with certain behaviors, such as using drugs or alcohol, sleeping, crying, or even impulsive shopping (Nist and Holschuh, 2002). What is your stress response? It is useful to be aware of your individual stress response so that you can better manage your symptoms. Here are some tried and true ways to begin to feel better when your world becomes a bit overwhelming:

- *Exercise.* If you are an athlete or adhere to a regular workout schedule, you already know how exercise can help soothe your body and mind. Exercise provides a healthy outlet for pent-up emotions and physical symptoms. Whatever you enjoy doing—jogging, swimming, bicycling, and so on—is beneficial. If you're not a regular exerciser, try a brisk 20-minute walk outdoors when you're feeling stressed. Take note of how you feel before and after the activity. You may be surprised!

- *Quiet time.* Sometimes the frantic pace of life and the incessant interruptions make it difficult to stop and pull yourself together. When you're feeling stressed, try to find a quiet place where you can be alone for a little while. Take time to relax, meditate, pray, or simply slow down your thoughts for a few minutes. When your body has had time to calm down, your mind can follow.

- *Journaling.* You are probably enduring many lifestyle changes now, are facing new stressors, and may have many questions and concerns regarding your immediate and long-term plans. Writing down your thoughts each night in a notebook may help you to make sense of your new world, express some feelings that you may not feel comfortable sharing with others, and engage in a process of self-reflection and creative problem solving.

- *Put things into perspective.* Sometimes the little things can build up and begin to feel more overwhelming than they actually are. A poor grade on a paper, a fight with a friend, and yet another parking ticket all in one morning may leave you feeling frustrated and ready to give up. Remind yourself that there is a solution and you can fix the problem; this, too, shall pass.

- *Take care of yourself.* When you can predict stressful times, such as finals week, job interviews, or perhaps the holiday season, be sure to eat properly, get adequate sleep, exercise, and avoid alcohol and caffeine. It is difficult to manage stress when our physical defenses are low.

- *See a counselor.* Finally, if you feel unable to cope with your stress on your own, contact your university counseling service. A trained and licensed professional can often help you to find the skills you need to effectively combat stress. If you've recently endured an extremely stressful event, such as the death of a good friend or family member, a divorce, or other personal crisis, please don't hesitate to seek help. Very few of us can cope with losses of large magnitudes by ourselves. Help is available!

How Much Sleep Do I Need?

As a student, you may be tempted to cut back on sleep in order to make time for the many obligations that you have every day. Sleep time is often the first thing to be sacrificed when we find that we cannot accomplish everything we want to. But as you may know, sleep deprivation is harmful: when you don't get enough sleep you will generally feel very tired and irritable, your reflexes will slow down (making it dangerous to drive), and your body's immune system can become compromised, thus increasing your vulnerability to illness. If you become sick, the time lost at work or in class may amount to more than the sleep you skipped.

How much sleep is enough? Adults generally need between six and eight hours each night. The sleep also needs to be continuous—in other words, four hours of sleep at night followed by a couple of cat naps during the day will usually not leave you feeling refreshed and well-rested. This is because our brains need to progress through several stages of sleep each night in order to reap the restorative benefits of a full night of rest. We begin in what is termed "quiet sleep," or a semiconscious dozing state from which we may be easily awakened. As we continue to sleep, we transcend to "active sleep," a very deep sleep, also known as "REM sleep." REM stands for "rapid eye movement," and is associated with the dreaming state. This is the state in which the brain receives the greatest rest and restoration. Young adults cycle through REM sleep about four times per night (Gleitman, 1996).

As tough as it may be, sleep should become an important priority for you. If you have budgeted enough time in your schedule for adequate sleep, but have trouble falling or staying asleep, here are a few tips that may help:

- Do not consume caffeine after 3 p.m.
- Reserve your bed for sleep only and retire at the same time each night. If you regularly use your bed to read, eat, or watch television at various times throughout the day, your body may not always get the message that it is time to go to sleep when you crawl under the covers at night.
- Daily exercise can help you to feel physically tired at the end of the day. However, be sure your workout is at least three hours before bedtime; otherwise, you may still be feeling too energized to sleep when bedtime arrives.
- Practice relaxing your entire body one part at a time as you try to fall asleep. Begin by consciously tensing, then relaxing your face muscles, then tense and relax your shoulders, then your hands, and so on until you are completely relaxed, from your eyebrows to your toes.

- Don't drink alcohol to help you sleep. Alcohol may help you fall asleep, but it ultimately interferes with normal sleep cycles and prevents you from feeling rested when you awaken.
- If insomnia persists, see your doctor. There may be a sleep aid available that will work to help you fall and stay asleep.

Is It Just the Blues, or Am I Really Depressed?

Good mental health means having a generally positive outlook on life, enjoying many of your daily activities, feeling optimistic about the future, and recovering relatively quickly when life's occasional frustrations or disappointments get you down. It is perfectly normal to feel sad, stressed, or angry from time to time—that's life! Nobody is in a good mood each and every day. But if you find yourself feeling sad, stressed, angry, or even hopeless much of the time, are generally not enjoying life, and cannot seem to break out of this pattern of feelings, then you may be suffering from emotional trauma that may need professional attention. Other signs of extreme stress or depression include changes in sleeping patterns, changes in eating patterns, loss of interest in activities you once enjoyed, isolation, or frequent bouts of tears. If these feelings or behaviors are all too familiar for you, call your university counseling center and talk to a professional immediately. If you notice a friend of family member exhibiting these feelings or behaviors, have a heart-to-heart talk and ask if they have sought help. If not, do what you can to encourage them to do so. Sometimes emotional problems are situational, and will resolve themselves over time, as you and your mental health professional work through them. Sometimes emotional problems are organic, meaning the symptoms are caused by a chemical imbalance in the brain. These imbalances can very often be successfully treated with medication. Sometimes the root of the problem is a combination of both organic and situational problems. Either way, a licensed professional can help.

One very common mental health issue on college campuses has to do with eating disorders. While it is important to be aware of our daily food choices and to strive for proper nutrition as much as possible, taken to an extreme, a normal conscientiousness about food can lead to an unhealthy obsession. If you feel preoccupied with food each day, have very strict rules about what types of food you may eat, and feel inordinately guilty if you violate those rules, you may have the symptoms of a serious eating disorder. About 30 percent of college students suffer from eating disorders (Litt, 2000). Although eating disorders are found predominately in women, men can develop them, too.

Eating disorders rarely begin intentionally. Our society celebrates a slim silhouette, and rejects chubbiness or obesity, thus reinforcing the collective desire to stay thin. Typically, a person may feel a reasonable need to diet, but over time, the dieting runs out of control. Early weight loss successes may fuel a sense of power, control, and superiority. A new sense of identity as a slim person emerges, and an obsession with controlling weight and appearance may become all-consuming. Disordered eating behaviors can become addictive and are difficult to overcome. Eating disorders can take one of several forms, and it is possible to suffer from a combination of these behaviors. Eating disorders can lead to many severe health problems, and the resulting complications can be fatal.

? Questions for Class Discussion

1. Is it easy or difficult for students to eat a healthy diet on our campus? Why?
2. How many of you have purchased a campus meal plan? Do you take advantage of healthy choices? Why or why not?
3. How many of you do not exercise as much as you should? What types of things keep you from exercising?
4. What is the role of alcohol or partying on our campus? How do you feel about college student alcohol use?
5. What can our administrators do to promote a healthier student lifestyle on our campus?
6. What can students do to encourage each other to eat right, exercise, and avoid abuse of alcohol or other substances?

Activity

What aspects of wellness do you find most challenging? Is it getting enough sleep, eating right, or limiting caffeine or alcohol? During the upcoming week, choose the health concern that you would most like to improve upon. Then keep a diary of your intake/substance use/sleep for the week. Identify ways that you can improve your lifestyle based on the content of this book chapter or other reliable sources that you find.

Next, create an ideal daily routine for yourself. Be as realistic as you can. Make it a priority to stick to your new routine—you may find you are soon feeling much more active and energized!

Journal Assignment

In your journal this week, reflect on the current state of your physical and mental health. Write one to two pages. To direct your writing, consider these questions:

1. If my body could talk to me about the way I care for it, what would it say? What kinds of changes would my body like to see happen?

2. Describe one adjustment to your lifestyle that you could implement tomorrow that would result in a positive change to your physical health.
3. What are the major sources of stress in my life?
4. What changes can I make in my lifestyle to help minimize or reduce these sources of stress?

Summary

- There is a strong relationship between good physical and mental health and overall success in college.
- Proper nutrition includes a balanced diet high in nutrients and low in trans fats, sugar, salt, and alcohol.
- Regular physical exercise is critical to maintaining a healthy weight, building strong bones and muscles, and to relieving stress.
- Abuse of alcohol can endanger you as well as others and will have a negative impact on your academic success.
- Six to eight hours of sleep each night is essential for optimal mental and physical functioning each day.
- Students should be aware of the state of their mental health and seek professional help when necessary.

Case Study

Juan had played the saxophone since junior high school, and had discovered that music performance was his passion in life. Juan was a talented musician, and had managed to maintain first chair status in his high school band for all four years. He also earned top honors at state competitions three years in a row. Juan was a very outgoing, confident, and personable young man, who enjoyed being with and helping others. During his senior year in high school, Juan identified an academic major and a career goal: Music Education, with the goal of becoming a high school band director.

Juan decided to complete his freshman year at an in-state college, and then transfer to an out of state school with an outstanding music program. Juan joined a small jazz band during his first year, and formed close friendships with his band mates. Although he enjoyed this group very much, he longed for more musical opportunities, particularly performing in a marching band.

Juan planned on getting involved in several musical ensembles at his new school, and looked forward to meeting new friends who shared his interests and goals. Juan auditioned for marching band and a wind ensemble, and was accepted for both. The wind ensemble was a small group, but the marching band was huge—more than 300 members!

During the first few weeks of the fall semester, Juan was overwhelmed with activities. Juan had a roommate in his residence hall room, but did not see him very much due to his busy schedule. He tried to initiate friendships with several of the students in the marching band and wind ensemble, but quickly discovered that these students had already formed their own cliques the previous year. Juan felt very much like an outsider.

Musically, Juan discovered that his level of talent was no longer exceptional relative to the other band members. Many of the other saxophone players at this new school were equally proficient, if not more so than Juan. Juan began to feel like a face in the crowd, no longer the shining star of the band.

By mid-term, Juan had given up on making new friends in the music department. He began sleeping a lot, and routinely skipped his early-morning classes. He found himself just wanting to be alone, and did his best to avoid contact with other people. He stopped dining in the school cafeteria, and instead survived on fast food that he could pick up and eat by himself. He began wondering if he had made the right decision about school, his major, and his career. When Juan went home for Thanksgiving, his family was alarmed to find that a silent, depressed, and now-overweight young man had taken the place of their once vibrant, outgoing, and self-confident son.

Food for Thought

What would you recommend Juan and his family do to help him feel better? Is Juan's reaction to the sequence of events to be expected? Why or why not?

Career Planning

8

[*"To find out what one is fitted to do, and to secure an opportunity to do it, is the key to happiness."*
—John Dewey]

In a Student's Voice

"This transfer experience thing is what you make of it. If you take the time and effort to talk to faculty and other students they will talk too, but you need to make the effort first. There are too many students here for every faculty member to know, but there are a lot of faculty and office people, so find one that you like and reach out to them."

—Erik, transfer student
(Nowak, 2004)

Learning Objectives

- Understand the relationship between academic interests and professional goals
- Discover opportunities in the current job market
- Understand the concept of self-marketing
- Identify valuable workplace skills
- Become familiar with the proper elements of a resume and cover letter
- Master the art of the professional interview

Quick Start Quiz

Assess your existing knowledge of key components of this chapter. Check each item below that applies to you:

- ❏   I have an academic major and/or a professional goal in mind.
- ❏   I am familiar with current trends in the job market.
- ❏   I have developed or know how to develop a resume.
- ❏   I know the basic skills that most employers seek.
- ❏   I understand how to interview successfully.

When Should I Begin Thinking About My Career?

If you're a transfer student, you know that the road from today to graduation is somewhat shorter than it is for new freshmen. That's good! But the pressure to create—and implement—your career plan is also on the rise. There's no time to lose—even if you have more than two years of course work ahead of you, the key to landing a great job *before* graduation day is to plan, prepare, and work hard toward your career goals. This chapter is designed to help!

Why focus on careers now? For starters, one of the primary factors in students' decisions to pursue a college degree is to expand employment options, and to elevate one's earning potential. Although a college degree does not guarantee a lucrative employment offer post-graduation, people with college degrees generally enjoy broader employment opportunities and can earn significantly more money over the course of a lifetime than those without a college degree. To make the most of your college education advantage, you'll need to establish your goals, take advantage of every opportunity to build your resume, and market yourself well. Fitting all of these tasks into your busy schedule can be a challenge. To help you visualize and manage your upcoming career preparation activities, a timeline for transfer students has been developed and is available as Appendix E in the back of this book.

Where Do I Begin?

What *is* your dream job? Some students come to college feeling very sure of their future career path, but for others this is not an easy question to answer! There are many, many directions to consider, yet many students have had limited opportunities to explore careers or have had limited exposure to the myriad of opportunities available.

The most important consideration is to find work that you will enjoy. Discover your passion and follow it! More on that a little later in this chapter. A second consideration—still very important, of course—is the job market. You may need to put steady employment and salary concerns near the top of your priority list, particularly if you are responsible for family members other than yourself. So if you are exploring career options, are open to new ideas, and need a great job quickly after graduation, consider the fields that are most likely to need new workers in the coming years.

Where Are the Jobs?

In *The Top 100: The Fastest Growing Careers for the 21st Century* (Ferguson, 2001), Health Services, Computers and Information Services, and Education are cited as the hottest career fields today. It's not hard to see why; our population is aging, thus requiring more health care; computers are a necessary fact of life for nearly all of us; and our growing population is becoming more and more educated. Opportunities in these fields generally require a four-year college degree, and are expected to grow faster than average through the year 2008 (Ferguson, 2001).

For further information on any of these occupations, as well as thousands more, help is just a click away. Check out up-to-date information on occupations, training required, salaries, and job outlook by visiting the U.S. Department of Labor's Occupational Outlook Handbook (http://www.bls.gov/oco/).

I Haven't Chosen a Major—What Should I Do?

If you have not yet decided on a major, it should be a pressing concern for you at this point in your academic career. While it is expected that freshmen will spend all or a portion of the first year of college exploring major options via general education course work, as students approach the middle of the sophomore year it may become difficult to continue to enroll in general education classes without also beginning to take classes required for the major. Also, many majors require specific sequencing of course work, thus prolonging the amount of time needed to complete the degree if the major course work is not initiated early in the academic career.

A portion of the course work required for many academic majors is designed to provide skills training for the particular career paths associated with the major. A few examples include accounting, medicine, engineering, and elementary education, among others. However, there are also a vast number of jobs available for college graduates that require the more general types of skills that students will obtain on any degree plan. These skills include written and verbal communication skills, problem-solving and critical thinking skills, personal responsibility, and the ability to set and achieve goals. These are the types of skills and abilities required of a vast number of professional positions. You will refine these types of essential skills during your college years regardless of your major. The more specific types of skills that you need for your particular job will often be gained via on-the-job training. The bottom line is this: aside from the more technical fields, such as accounting or engineering, your college education, regardless of major, will provide you with skills employers seek and will prepare you for a wide range of career paths.

If choosing a major is a priority for you now, there are steps you can take to get the process started. First and foremost, consider what you love to learn. Your college course work is generally not a rigid roadmap to your future career, but is rather your opportunity to refine your skills via in-depth study of a topic that you enjoy. Consider the classes you have already completed, and those you are enrolled in now. Which ones pique your interest? Which ones do you look forward to studying and reading about? Alternatively, which ones do you dislike? Using the process of elimination can also be an effective way to narrow down your major choices.

Many students find that there are two or three different disciplines that are of interest. If this is the case for you, talk to your academic advisor about combining more than one major, or combining a major and a minor. There may also be multidisciplinary majors and/or minors available at your school. A multidisciplinary major allows you to customize your studies by combining several areas of interest. Remember, your choice of major is not necessarily tied to a lifelong career. Choosing a major is about choosing what you love to learn about!

Still feeling undecided? Try this. Pretend you are 75 years old, and are reflecting back on your life. You enjoyed a very fulfilling and rewarding career, and had become quite famous. During the course of your career, you had solved a critical world problem, or had provided the answer to a very complex question. Ask yourself, *what was that problem or question?* The answer may reflect upon your strongest passions and values, and may help point you in the direction of an academic major that you will find interesting and rewarding to study. If you are not sure how to connect these values and interests with a major at your school, contact your academic advisor for assistance.

If, after some serious soul-searching and exploration on your own, you still feel quite undecided about your major, there are resources on your campus to assist you. Your career planning center will offer various types of assessments to help you clarify your interests, values, and lifestyle preferences that will connect to appropriate majors and careers. Assessment results can offer you new ideas to consider or may confirm what you already know you enjoy. Assessment results are useful, but they are not a crystal ball, and cannot guarantee success or happiness in any particular field.

For some students, however, no amount of information or exploration is quite enough to get to the point where a decision can comfortably and confidently be made. When this appears to be the case, an individual meeting with a professional career or personal counselor at your school may be in order. A professional counselor can help you to uncover and possibly resolve any personal or emotional issues that may be hindering the decision-making process.

Do What You Love and the Money Will Follow

You have probably heard this saying before, but is it really true? A study conducted by Mark Albion suggests that it is. This researcher surveyed 1500 college graduates and asked them if their first job was selected on the basis of salary (group one) or whether their first job was selected because they felt passionate about the work, regardless of the salary (group two). About 83 percent, or 1245 of the respondents, fell into group one, and about 17 percent, or 255, fell into group two.

These respondents were contacted again 20 years later. At that point, 101 of the respondents had become multimillionaires. Of those 101 individuals, only one was a member of group one, having originally chosen a job based on salary. The remaining 100 were members of group two, those who had followed their passions (Albion, 2000). These data suggest that *success is most likely to come to those who truly love what they do every day!*

Can I Really "Market" Myself?

Now that you have established your goal, it is time to begin *marketing yourself.* Thousands of students graduate from college each year, and it is up to you to set yourself apart and sell your unique set of talents to employers. You will be getting involved on campus, earning related work experience, and building your leadership, communication, and other important skills so that employers will want to hire *you,* and not someone else! It may seem odd to think of marketing a person, the same way that cars or laundry soap are sold, but in reality the process is quite similar. Think about the last time you went shopping for a pair of tennis shoes. You went to the store, tried on a few pairs of shoes, and perhaps narrowed it down to a pair of Nike shoes and a pair of Adidas shoes. Both pairs of shoes were high-quality products, with a few differences in color, features, and price. Either pair would adequately meet your footwear needs. The decision that you made rested on the small details that were most important to you.

The same scenario plays out when you interview for a job. An employer will make a hiring decision based upon the applicant who has the most experiences, skills, and traits that are the very best fit for the position. Your job is to find out what the employer wants, and make sure you can offer it better than anyone else. This is essentially "marketing" your person and all that comes with it to the company.

A final thought: in order to successfully market yourself to an employer, you must first successfully market yourself to *you*. If you are not confident in yourself, how can an employer feel confident about you? As Joe Girard points out in *How to Sell Yourself* (1979), "You must believe in yourself, have faith in yourself and have confidence in yourself. In short, you must be totally aware of your own self-worth." To foster self-confidence, Girard recommends that you hang out with other confident people, and avoid associating with slackers; give yourself a pat on the back every day; and tell yourself each morning, "I am my own best salesperson!"

What Do Employers Want?

Employers have described several types of essential skills that they look for in job applicants. As described earlier, these are skills that most college graduates should possess as a result of college course work and experiences, regardless of major. Santrock and Halonen (2004) identified the following areas of interest for most employers. Ask yourself if you are already proficient in each area, or if you will need to work on any of these skill areas.

- *Speaking skills*—are you an articulate speaker? Do you have a well-rounded vocabulary? Are you poised and confident speaking in front of a group?
- *Interpersonal skills*—do you relate well to others? Are you approachable and pleasant? Do you look others in the eye when speaking to them?
- *Analytical skills*—when given several pieces of information, can you break them down and identify patterns? Can you organize and interpret the information?
- *Teamwork skills*—do you work well in a group? Do you contribute to the project without relying heavily on others? Do you work cooperatively and productively with team members?
- *Flexibility*—do you adapt well to change? Can you shift gears in the middle of a project? Can you adjust your working style or schedule when needed?

- *Leadership skills*—can you direct a group project? Do you motivate others well? Can you delegate tasks when necessary?
- *Writing skills*—do you express yourself well on paper? Are your spelling and grammar skills up to par? Are you adept at formal writing, such as research papers or business correspondence?
- *Computer skills*—are you proficient with common applications such as word processing, spreadsheets, databases, Internet, and e-mail?

If you could not answer "yes" to all of the questions above, consider ways to seek out experiences that will improve your skills in each area. Volunteering for an executive position in student government or student organizations is one way to improve in many of the areas, particularly leadership, interpersonal skills, and teamwork. A course in computer applications, speech communication, or advanced grammar may help in some of the other areas.

How Do I Build My Resume?

You might have heard the phrase, "You need to have a job to get a job." In many respects, it's true! Employers want to hire employees who have related work experience. It is in the employer's best interest to hire someone who has not only demonstrated an ability to perform the skills needed on the job, but to also hire someone who has demonstrated an ability to approach the workplace in a professional, mature, ethical, and responsible manner. Your college education provides the foundation for success, but you'll need real-world, concrete experience in your chosen field in order to be competitive in today's job market.

Fortunately, there are many opportunities to gain related work experience while you are in school. Ideally, you'll find an experience that will build the skills and abilities that you'll use in your chosen profession. If you do not find something that is directly related to your future career, try to find something that will help refine the general skills that are valuable to employers, such as leadership, teamwork, verbal or written communication, punctuality, and professionalism. It is important to note that work experience is important to your prospective employer because it provides evidence that you are familiar with a business environment, that you understand the value of punctuality and productivity. Those things alone put you ahead of others without such experience. Here is a list of some employment possibilities to explore. Chances are you may not have large blocks of time in your busy schedule to add these types of experiences, yet these types of experiences are priceless in terms of preparing you for your first job.

Your academic advisor or career planning office can offer you contact information for each of the following:

- *Part-time paid employment on- or off-campus.* If you can find work directly or indirectly related to your career goal, this is the perfect resume builder. You will be gaining valuable experience while paying the bills, too. If you're having trouble finding permanent paid employment, try contacting a temporary employment agency. Job assignments through these agencies may vary from a few days to a few months.

- *Volunteer or community service experience.* Experience is always valuable whether or not a paycheck is attached! Every campus and community will have ample opportunities for volunteerism. If you're not sure where to look for these opportunities, check with your academic advisor.

- *Internships.* Internships are like part-time jobs (often full-time in the summer) related to your career goal. Internships are sometimes paid, but often are not. Employers will often hire interns to perform many routine job tasks while acquainting the intern with the functions and culture of the company. But the experience will pay off down the road—internships can often result in a permanent job with the company after graduation! If you cannot be paid for your efforts, ask about receiving college credit instead. In many cases, companies require students to receive academic credit for internship work for which they are not being paid to comply with federal rules governing wage and hour requirements.

- *Summer jobs.* If you're not taking classes during the summer term, consider a full-time job related to your career interests. Check with your campus career planning center to investigate job postings or career fairs.

- *Student organizations/student government.* Leadership experience can be found right on campus! Get involved in a student club or organization related to your career interests as soon as you can. An executive position such as president, vice president, or treasurer is especially valuable.

- *Assistantships.* It may be possible to obtain a teaching or research assistantship in your academic department. Contact your advisor or a professor with whom you would like to work to explore your options.

Your resume is more than just a summary of your education and experiences; it can be thought of as an "advertisement" for yourself. Your resume is a critical marketing tool when it comes time to apply for internships, part-time work, or full-time work upon graduation. It must portray your set of skills and experiences in the best light possible. Your resume must be flawless, engaging, accurate, truthful, and, when appropriate, artistic. Employers are known to eliminate applicants based on a single typo; attention to detail will be critical. Do not misrepresent yourself on your resume—if you do land the job, intentional inaccuracies may be grounds for termination later.

It is important to create and maintain your resume early in your college career. You may need a resume to apply for part-time jobs in college, or to apply for certain scholarships. Keeping your resume up to date will help you to write clear and accurate descriptions of your employment and extracurricular experiences—if you wait until the last minute to develop your resume, it may be difficult to remember the details of each experience that you have had. Also, creating a resume quickly is likely to result in errors, omissions, and poor word choices. Give yourself time to write, and revise, revise, revise. Ask a professor, advisor, or career professional at your school for feedback on your resume.

Many employers request or require applicants to apply online, and to send an electronic copy of the resume and cover letter. In these cases, a "pdf" version of your resume will help to preserve the formatting and any artistic elements in your documents.

Your resume will include certain basic information about yourself. Keep in mind that after your freshman year in college, high school information and activities are no longer relevant and should not be included on your resume. In general, a complete resume should include:

- *Contact information.* This is your name, address, telephone number(s), and e-mail address. If you have an answering machine or voice mail service for your cell phone, be sure that your outgoing message is brief, personal, and professional. A generic message, such as "You have reached 555-1234; please leave a message," can also be frustrating to the caller because there is no indication that the caller has reached the proper voice mailbox. "You have reached the voice mailbox of Angela Adams. Your call is very important to me. Please leave a message after the tone and I will return your call shortly," is an example of a brief, personal, and professional message. By the same token, be sure that your e-mail address is also a professional, personal, nonoffensive sequence of words or characters.
- *Objective.* The objective statement matches your skills and experience with the necessary qualifications for the job you are pursuing. It can be modified for each specific job application. A word of warning: it is very easy to accidentally send a resume for Job B with an objective written for Job A; this is an embarrassing situation, to say the least. Be sure to double-check your objective if you are sending out resumes for multiple types of jobs.
- *Education.* Again, high school information is no longer relevant. Include the title of the college degree you intend to receive, as well as the name

of your school and the anticipated graduation date. If you are anticipating a graduate or professional degree, do not put the title of the program on your resume until you have applied to and have been accepted to the program.

- *Experience.* Depending upon the nature of the experiences you have had, you may approach this section in several different ways. You may have paid work experience, volunteer experience, or experience that you earned via college credit (for example, a teaching or research assistantship). Summarize the responsibilities of each position, including what you accomplished in the position, briefly in either paragraph or bullet form. The format of your resume will also dictate how this section is approached.

- *Activities.* This section would include membership in student clubs or organizations, student government, honor societies, fraternity or sorority, and community service work.

- *Honors and Awards.* If you have received a merit-based scholarship, have made the dean's list for one or more semesters, or have any type of special recognition that you earned in college, it is appropriate to list under this type of heading.

- *Special Skills.* Cite your computer skills, including the type of hardware and software you are familiar with in this section. Other skills that would be appropriate include fluency in a second language, typing speed, or any licenses or certifications that you may have. Special skills should be related to academia or to the workplace—do not include leisure-related skills, such as computer games, hobbies, or sports.

I've Seen All Kinds of Resumes; What Format Is Best for Me?

A variety of resume formats is available. The three most common formats are the chronological resume, the functional resume, and the combination resume. Examples of each are included in Appendix F.

The chronological resume is by far the most common and straightforward format. Work experiences are simply listed in reverse chronological order, starting with the current or most recent position. This format is appropriate when your experiences are closely related to the new position you are seeking. The advantage to using this format is that it is very easy for an employer to scan your resume quickly and determine whether or not your experiences and skills are a good match for the position.

The functional resume summarizes skills and accomplishments, and relates those to the intended career goal. If you are a nontraditional or returning student, your life experiences may fit this format well. A student would choose this format if there are gaps in work history, or if you are a career changer, and your current or previous job titles do not clearly connect to the desired field or position. This format enables you to highlight your abilities and skills acquired in a variety of settings, such as school, volunteerism, homemaking, or personal hobbies.

The combination resume uses elements from both the chronological and functional resumes. It is very useful for highlighting accomplishments and skills that may have been gleaned via a variety of different work, volunteer, or educational experiences. It is appropriate for students who could opt for the chronological resume, but would like to bring the reader's attention to a specific set of skills that directly relate to the position sought.

A college student or new college graduate's resume should usually be limited to one page. Generally employers will not read every word, but will rather skim the document for highlights. For additional detail and guidance, many books are available on the subject of writing resumes. Your school's career planning or career services office is likely to have several books available for you to borrow, or check your college library.

On Your Campus

Identify your career development, planning, or services office (the office on your campus may have any of a number of names). Make an appointment with a career services staff member to discuss your plans for employment after graduation and relevant campus activities or opportunities that will enhance your marketability.

What About the Cover Letter?

The cover letter is a document that accompanies your resume. It is an additional opportunity to market yourself, and to provide information detailing your interest in the job, why you are seeking a job, and any additional relevant facts that you would want the employer to know. Avoid noninformative cover letters that simply state the job that you are seeking and that your resume is attached; this may suggest to the employer that you are not genuinely interested in the position. The letter should be addressed to the individual making the hiring decision, if one is specified. As with the resume, your cover letter must be written with flawless spelling and grammar, professionalism, and truthfulness. It should also be limited to one page. Employers do not want to read your entire life story! That said, it can sometimes be a challenge to include everything you wish the employer to know in such limited space. Therefore, follow these guidelines:

- Limit your letter to three paragraphs.
- The first paragraph is the *opening*, in which you explain why you are writing. State the exact title of the position you seek.
- The second paragraph is the *body*, in which you explain why you are an exceptional candidate for the job based on your background and experiences. Don't repeat everything on your resume; focus on the highlights. Strive to convince the reader that you are an ideal candidate, but be humble—avoid arrogance or conceit.
- The final paragraph is the *closing*, in which you convey how and when you can be reached, and emphasize your enthusiasm for the job (Hawk, 1998).

In summary, be brief, be direct, be assertive, but be humble. An example of each type of resume and a cover letter are provided in Appendix F.

As your resume begins to take shape, begin thinking about the next step: getting your resume out there! The job search begins many months in advance, not the day after graduation. The job search requires a high level of initiative, attention to detail, and organizational skills. You'll need to use several search methods; make sure every resume and cover letter that goes out reflects your best work; and keep track of the jobs for which you've applied.

Begin with your career planning office. There may be special programs or partnerships especially for students at your school that can help you with your job search skills and help you to connect with employers. These services may include on-campus career fairs and recruiting programs; online resume posting; mock interviews; resume help; alumni networks; and internship and job listings. Take advantage of all that you can; it is there for you!

How Do I Prepare for an Interview?

The interview is a critical opportunity to once again market yourself and your talents, skills, and personality. Unfortunately, many job interviews do not go smoothly because the candidate was not prepared, was too nervous, or did not approach the interview in a professional and appropriate manner.

One of the most important aspects of the interview is professional dress. The first impression that the employer will have of you is how you are dressed and groomed. Your professionalism, maturity, and judgment are reflected in your clothes and overall appearance. A professional suit and appropriate shoes will be a worthwhile investment. Conservative colors such as grey, navy, or black are safe choices. Minimize jewelry. If you have an observable body piercing, you should remove it. Be sure your hair has been recently cut and is well-groomed.

A second very important step to a successful interview is to research the employer. Find out all that you can about the company's history, products, services, personnel, market share, and competitors. Your knowledge of the company and its market sector will convey your interest in the job and your seriousness about this particular opportunity.

Like everything else in life, it takes practice to master the art of the job interview. It is rarely possible to know exactly what to expect. You may be interviewed by one person or a group of ten people. Your interview may last 20 minutes or two hours. The questions may be predictable or they may be tricky. You may have just one interview for a particular position, or several interviews.

However, there are steps that you can take to help prepare yourself as much as humanly possible. In this section we'll discuss some basic tips for successful job interviews.

Interview Tips for Nontraditional Students

Are you in college now due to a radical career change? Are you returning to school after a long break? Will you be older than 40 on graduation day? Do you have a physical disability? All of these circumstances may lead you to feel less than competitive in the job market with your twenty-something classmates. However, there are several ways that you can use your unique circumstances to your advantage during the interview.

Think about what your unique life experiences have taught you. These experiences can give you an edge in the interview, if you market yourself well. For example, consider this career-changer. Mary was trained as a hairdresser, and worked at a salon for many years while raising her children. She is now in college majoring in business administration. How can her many years of experience cutting hair help prepare her for a management position? For starters, she learned to make conversation and get along with many different types of clients. People skills are critical in management. Secondly, she understood her role in marketing the salon—an expertly coiffed client can send many new customers her direction. Marketing is also a critical function in business.

Or consider Henry, who has taken a long break from college and will be older than his classmates' parents on graduation day. Henry may be able to market several unique talents simply by virtue of his birth date. Employees over 50 often work harder, stay with the company longer, are more productive, more patient, and have better attitudes than their younger colleagues (Helfand, 1995).

continued

Younger people are more likely to be impulsive, take risks, have accidents, and make mistakes simply due to lack of experience. If you have wrinkles, consider them well-earned.

Finally, if you have a physical disability, consider all of the challenges you have overcome to accomplish your goals. Certainly you have demonstrated persistence, patience, confidence, and resourcefulness to be where you are today. Communicate these talents to your prospective employers, and you can earn their respect.

What Is the Employer Thinking During an Interview?

Employers conduct interviews to collect information that a resume cannot completely provide. In order to determine if you are the best person for the job, employers will want to know three basic things:

1. Do you possess the education, skills, and abilities to perform the job well?
2. What is your personality like? What traits and characteristics define you? Will you get along with your colleagues?
3. Will you be part of the problem or part of the solution? (Porot, 1999)

The first concern, regarding your ability to perform the job, is probably the most straightforward of the three. You can prepare for questions relating to your skills and abilities by carefully reading the job announcement, and creating a list of examples from your past experiences that relate to the activities required for the new job. Remember, be specific, and cite as many detailed examples as you can.

The second concern relates to your general personality and people skills. Are you outgoing and talkative, or shy and reserved? Do you tend to take the lead in group discussions, or are you a listener? Are you tolerant of points of view other than your own, or do you tend to persuade others to share your perspective? The employer will be looking for clues as to how well you will get along with the others in your work group, and how well you will fit in with the overall company culture.

The final concern relates to your expected overall performance in the job. Will you learn the job quickly or need quite a bit of training and supervision? Will you be a loyal employee for many years or quit after a few months? Will you help boost morale in your unit or cause distress? Employers are seeking employees who are productive, dependable, and pleasant. Consider examples from your past that will assuage any of these concerns that the interviewer may have.

Don't forget that the job interview is also *your* chance to interview the employer! The employment arrangement needs to be a mutually beneficial match for both you and the company. Your needs, goals, and preferences in the workplace are very important to consider. The interviewer will generally ask if you have any questions for him or her toward the end of the interview. You can impress the interviewer if you have three or four thoughtful, relevant questions prepared. For example, did something about the company's history pique your interest as you did your research before the interview? Are you interested in learning more about training or professional development opportunities? Stay away from questions about the salary, however; that topic is usually most appropriate at the time an offer is made. The employer will want to feel assured that your interest in the job extends beyond the paycheck!

Please see the figure below for common questions that interviewers may ask, and a few ideas for questions of your own.

Questions to Ask and Answer

Commonly Asked Interview Questions

- Tell me about yourself. (Focus on your accomplishments as they relate to the job.)
- Why do you want to work here? (Use your research about the organization/position to reply.)
- What are your strengths? Weaknesses? (Relate them to performing the job.)
- What are your goals? (Connect this job to your career plan and/or calling.)
- Describe your most significant professional accomplishment. Your biggest challenge. (Relate these experiences to attributes you bring to this position.)
- What job did you like best? Least? (This is not the time to be hypercritical of former employers or supervisors.)
- What is your work style? What type supervision do you prefer?
- Does your GPA accurately reflect your abilities?

Questions You Might Ask

- Request clarification about particular aspects of the job; e.g., typical day/week, reporting relationships, learning opportunities, organizational structure, etc.
- How would you describe the company's mission and management philosophy?
- How are people evaluated in the organization?
- Is there a typical career path in this area of the organization?
- What are the essential factors for success in this position?
- What are the challenges of this position?
- Where are you in the search process? What are the next steps?

Finally, although a job interview is anxiety-provoking for almost anyone, there are steps you can take to help boost your self-confidence and ease those interview jitters. First, prepare for the interview. Learn all that you can about the company. Think of the questions that you have for the interviewer. Review your resume and be prepared to answer questions about each of your experiences. Try on your interview clothes to be sure everything is clean, pressed, and fits.

Next, be sure to get a good night's sleep before your interview day, eat sensibly, and avoid excessive caffeine. On your way to the interview, breathe deeply, relax, and tell yourself, "I am my own best salesperson!" *And smile!*

After the interview, be sure to write a thank you letter. It is appropriate to repeat your interest in the position, and to thank the interviewer(s) for their time. If all goes well, a job offer may be on its way to you! If you do not get the offer, realize that it may take some time to land the right job, and that persistence is critical. As Thomas Edison once said, "I've not failed. I've just found 10,000 ways that won't work." You may want to reflect on what you felt went well in the interview, and what did not go well. Again, it will take practice to master the art of the interview. Don't give up, make adjustments where necessary, and above all, don't lose your self-confidence!

Should I Consider Graduate School?

Although a bachelor's degree is adequate preparation for entry into many fields, an advanced degree is required for some occupations. For example, licensed mental health therapists, attorneys, dentists, and college professors are professionals who have the required advanced degree in their fields. If your ultimate career goal does require an advanced degree, and you are willing to continue your education, please read on! If you are not sure what your ultimate objective is, however, and are considering graduate school because you enjoy school and would simply like to continue, invest some time now into refining your career goals so that you choose the most appropriate program for your future professional interests. Unlike many undergraduate degrees, graduate degree programs are typically profession- or discipline-specific.

Many students choose to take a break from school and gain related work experience before beginning graduate study. This can be extremely helpful in several ways: you will build your resume, thus demonstrating to graduate admissions committees your commitment to your field; you will confirm for yourself your interests and goals; you will gain a professional perspectives and experiences that will benefit your future studies; and you may be able to save some needed cash for graduate school tuition and expenses.

If you decide to continue your education immediately after completing your undergraduate degree, however, advance planning is critical for successful and timely admission to graduate school. You will want to research available and suitable programs in your field. Your criteria will vary depending upon your field and type of degree sought, but should generally include quality and reputation of the program, research interests of faculty, costs and available financial aid, and location. Most programs will require admissions test scores, letters of recommendation, a personal statement, resume, and transcripts, all well in advance of matriculation. You may see deadlines as early as December or January for the upcoming fall term. It is never too early to beginning planning. Meet with a faculty member in your chosen discipline for guidance in this process.

? Questions for Class Discussion

1. How many of you have career goals in mind?
2. For those of you with goals established, how did you come to your decision?
3. Does the idea of "marketing yourself" sound difficult? Why or why not?
4. What experiences are you seeking or do you already have related to your goal?
5. Should college graduates be guaranteed jobs? Why or why not?
6. What is the most challenging piece of the job search?

Activity

Do you have a Facebook or MySpace account? Check to be sure you are presenting yourself professionally. Omit any photos or references to activities that are illegal, or may be perceived as unethical or undesirable in an employee. Why? A recent survey by the National Association of Colleges and Employers indicates that about 27 percent of employers check social networking sites or Google the names of job applicants (National Association of Colleges and Employers, 2006). Silly party pictures or references to questionable activities or hobbies may cost you a job offer.

Journal Assignment

Imagine you are interviewing for your dream job. Reflect upon your traits, abilities, and experiences that have prepared you for this job. Consider how you might answer the following common interview questions:

1. Describe your most outstanding achievement to date.
2. What are your strengths and what are your weaknesses?
3. How do you spend your spare time?
4. Why should I hire you?

Summary

- Career planning should begin early in one's college career.
- Familiarity with the current job market can help define career goals.
- Academic majors are not necessarily directly tied to professional positions.
- Students should understand how to gain necessary experiences to market themselves effectively.
- A high-quality resume and cover letter are critical to the job search process.
- Mastering the art of the interview is also critical to land the job.

Case Study

Toshi was a college senior, just two months shy of graduating with his marketing degree. His goal for the past two years had been to have a job waiting for him upon graduation—after all, he was paying his own way and the student loans would come due quickly. Toshi chose to pursue a career in pharmaceutical sales. He felt confident that he would be able to earn the relevant academic, employment, and extracurricular experience that would make him an ideal job candidate.

Toshi worked hard to build his resume during college. He worked part-time in retail sales during the school year, and accepted a full-time position in outside sales the summer before senior year. In addition, he was elected vice president of the Marketing Club junior year, and president the following year. To assist in his understanding of pharmaceuticals and human physiology, Toshi earned minors in both biology and chemistry. His grades weren't perfect, given his course work and his busy schedule, but he felt confident he could "sell" himself to prospective employers.

Toshi worked closely with his career planning office to get help with his resume, network with alumni, and register to meet with recruiters during campus visits. Everything went according to plan, and Toshi landed an interview with a top pharmaceutical company just a few weeks before graduation. He was elated. He knew now that he had played his cards right.

Toshi knew a lot about sales, and felt comfortable in his ability to sell himself. He felt so comfortable, in fact, that he did not really prepare for the interview. Toshi was an energetic, outgoing, and very talkative person. He expected the interview to be stress-free.

During the interview, however, Toshi was taken a bit by surprise. He was asked questions that he did not anticipate. Here's how it went:

Interviewer: "Toshi, as you know, our firm has an excellent reputation in the pharmaceuticals field. Tell us what you know about us and how your skills match our needs."

Toshi was stunned. He had done no research on the company. He recognized the name, of course, but was unprepared to discuss the firm in any detail. He was forced to be quite vague in his answer.

Toshi: "Uh, yes, your firm is definitely the leader in the field. My experience and skill in sales will certainly help you maintain your position. I am confident that I can help you do that."

Interviewer: "OK. Well, as you probably also know, we are interviewing 12 students over the course of this week and next for two positions. Tell me why we should hire you."

Toshi: "Well, because I'm the best! (laughs) I will tell you right now I can outsell anybody on campus. No one can match me—I'm the superhero of sales! (laughs again)

Interviewer: "OK. Describe for us your greatest strength and your greatest weakness."

Toshi: "My greatest strength? Sure! I can persuade anybody to buy anything. Last summer I was the top salesperson in the entire company for the month of July. And I was not even out of school yet—I trumped a lot of old guys."

Interviewer: "And your greatest weakness?"

Toshi: "Weakness? Well, I don't have a weakness. I am the superhero of sales, don't you know?"

Sadly, Toshi's lack of preparation, arrogance, and inappropriate use of humor cost him the job.

Food for Thought

How might Toshi have better prepared for the interview? How might he have responded when he was unprepared for a question? Was there anything he could have done to save the interview?

Your Next Transition: The First Year After College

9

In a Student's Voice

"The academics are definitely to a higher degree than I experienced at community college. At community college a lot of the students were just there to appease their parents, because they didn't know what they wanted to do, or just didn't get into other schools. Here at the university I am surrounded by other very intelligent people that want to learn, and intellectuals, and professors that have their terminal degrees and what not. And I would say, that has been a big influence on my overall academic success. Because I feel like just being around these people has inspired me more, and kind of spurred me on. Since arriving here I've accomplished what I never thought I would have. I never thought I'd ever, in my life, make a Dean's List at a college, and I did. I mean, this semester I'm doing excellent."

—Andrew, transfer student
(Nowak, 2004)

Learning Objectives

- Understand the differences between college and the work environment
- Become familiar with employer expectations for professional appearance and behavior
- Learn how to identify and work with a mentor
- Understand the role of teamwork and coworker relationships
- Learn to embrace diversity in the workplace
- Consider the challenges and rewards of entrepreneurship

Quick Start Quiz

Assess your existing knowledge of key components of this chapter. Check each item below that applies to you:

- ❏   I am familiar with the differing expectations in school and in the workplace.
- ❏   I know how to seek and work with a professional mentor.
- ❏   I understand the principles of professional behavior and communication.
- ❏   I feel confident in my ability to manage conflict in groups.
- ❏   I understand the importance of diversity in the workplace.

What Will My First Year on the Job Be Like?

Whether graduation day is one, two, or three years out, it will be a banner day for you, and one of your most important accomplishments to date. Indeed, your college diploma is a key that can open many new doors for you. But your college diploma cannot guarantee a successful and productive professional career. There are many issues to consider and important attitudes to embrace as you enter the next phase of your life.

Your first job after graduation may be your first professional position ever, or you may be changing careers as a result of your recent college education and training. In either case, you will be entering a new environment as a learner, a rookie, a newbie. Yes, in many respects your first year on the job will be a transitional year—all over again!

Your first job after graduation from college will be just that—your first job. It is not uncommon for new college graduates to find that their *ideal* first position is just out of reach. It may be necessary to take a job as a stepping stone to that preferred position—some call it "paying our dues." Don't feel discouraged if you need to spend the first year or two in an entry-level job refining the skills and experiences that you need to be competitive for the job you really want.

Your first year on the job will undoubtedly be one of adjustment, challenges, and new experiences, in many ways similar to your first year of college or this first year at your current institution. The first year out will be a year of learning, listening, asking questions, and seeking guidance. And a strong, successful first year on the job will be critical to your continued success. Often people have trouble making the adjustment, but that should not deter you from your overall mission. If you struggle during your first year out, you will need to muster the confidence, resilience, and self-reliance to get up, brush yourself off, and start all over again. This chapter will help to acquaint you with some of the issues you will encounter as you enter or re-enter the world of work, help you to identify strategies for professional success, help prepare you for a productive and rewarding start to your new career.

One of the comforts of being a student in the classroom is feeling informed, for the most part, of exactly what is expected of you. As you know, your syllabus for each course describes the course content and objectives, the assignments, the schedule and assignment deadlines, and what you must accomplish to earn an "A" in the course. When you have questions, your instructor is available to answer them. If you follow the instructions, meet all of the requirements, and work diligently, it is usually within your power to do well in the course.

At work, as in life, however, there is no syllabus. It is unwise to assume expectations will be communicated clearly, and that regular feedback will occur. Often supervisors and colleagues are not very specific at all when communicating expectations. They may assume that you have knowledge and skills that you may or may not have. They may have been with the organization so long that many procedures or tasks that are brand new to you may be second nature to them. You may not readily know what is expected of you, or even what questions to ask. You may find yourself working with minimal or inconsistent direction and feedback. On the job, hard work does not always get recognized or result in a promotion.

If your first weeks or months on the job include a formal training program, by all means rejoice and consider yourself blessed. If new employee training is informal, brief, or nonexistent in your organization, however, then you will need to consider the following strategies to help you survive the first few weeks and months.

- *Be sure that you have a current, detailed, and complete description of your position.* Read it carefully and ask your supervisor about any responsibilities that are unclear, or that were not mentioned in the job interview. Employers often use a position description as a template for future performance reviews. You are likely to be evaluated on each and every aspect of your job, whether or not you received any training or instructions on how to perform each function.
- *Get to know a coworker in a similar position or level who has been with the organization for at least a year.* Ask questions about his or her experiences during the first year, and try to learn from his or her mistakes. Ask about the aspects of the job that have been the most rewarding and the most frustrating for this person. What would this employee do differently if he or she had the first year to do over again?
- *Ask for regular feedback from your supervisor.* Some supervisors are very good about providing regular feedback on employee performance; some are not. It can be devastating to learn about mistakes you have made months after the fact, or worse, hear about them for the first time in an annual performance review. Alternatively, it can be very rewarding to

know you are doing a great job! And if not, be grateful for any constructive criticism that you may receive, so that you can adjust your work accordingly and demonstrate success.

If you begin to feel overwhelmed or frustrated during your first few months on the job, remember that this transition to work—just like your transition from one school to another—will be challenging in many different ways. There may be times you become so frustrated that you feel like quitting. Unless the situation is unbearable, try not to quit. It will be critical to keep your cool, seek the help that you need, and stick it out for at least a year. It may be difficult to land another job, or to advance in your career, if you are perceived as a "job hopper."

Workplace Trends for the 21st Century

In *Change Your Job, Change Your Life*, Ron Krannich (2002) identifies several workplace trends for the 21st century that new college graduates would be wise to pay attention to! As you begin to consider your long-term professional goals and lifestyle preferences, keep in mind that:

- Fewer young people will be available for entry-level jobs as the baby boomer generation hits middle age and the U.S. birth rate slows to a stop. As a result, more entry-level opportunities may be available for new college graduates or for career changers.
- The Southwest, Northwest, and Florida will grow in population and wealth at the expense of the Northeast and North Central regions of the U.S. Economic indicators suggest that more job opportunities will be available in these regions, especially in the fields of construction and government.
- Ninety percent of all new jobs will be new small businesses. This will result in an increase in innovation and competition, and job opportunities, especially in Internet or service-based businesses.
- Many workers will change jobs every four years or so. The Internet has made job seeking more convenient, and employers have made retirement plans more portable, thus rendering the decision to advance or change careers less time consuming and financially punitive.
- Health care and high-tech careers will offer the best pay, security, and opportunity for advancement in the coming decades. Given the wide variety of occupations within these industries, you may want to investigate your options!
- In order to recruit and retain quality employees, many employers may offer added incentives, such as signing bonuses, options to work from home, profit-sharing packages, relocation reimbursements, flexible hours, and day care.

Do I Need a Mentor?

Without your college professors and advisors, you may feel that you've lost the support, feedback, and guidance that you once had and valued—all at a time when your world has once again changed dramatically. A "mentor" can help you adapt to the new organizational culture, develop the skills you need to succeed on the job, learn more about yourself, and prepare to move forward in your career. Some employers have formal mentoring programs, but many do not. It may be completely up to you to identify a mentor and establish an ongoing mentoring relationship, but it can be a very valuable and helpful endeavor.

As you get to know your more seasoned colleagues, be looking for those who may be in a position to mentor you. Here are a few tips to help you identify a good mentor:

- Look for someone with an excellent reputation in the company, and whose knowledge, skills, and career path are related to your interests and ambitions.
- Consider how your skills and ideas may benefit the mentor. Mentorship is a two-way street, and your prospective mentor may be looking for fresh ideas or renewed energy in one of his or her projects. He or she may even delegate an important project to you, thus affording you an opportunity to demonstrate your talents, creativity, and resourcefulness.
- Look for someone who will have the time and interest in mentoring you. An employee who frequently must travel out of town for several days at a time, or has many family obligations outside of the workplace, may have difficulty making time for you.
- As you narrow down the possible list of mentors, consider your personalities, communication styles, and level of trust with each other. As in all relationships, these issues can make a difference.

If you are not able to identify a mentor at work, consider seeking a mentor via other organizations such as a professional society or community service groups. Once you have identified a mentor, be sure to have a frank and honest discussion about the expectations of the relationship that each of you have, as well as how frequently and in what context you will interact with one another. The relationship that you establish may only be active for a year or so, or it may last a lifetime.

Networking

Networking is the process of developing and maintaining professional relationships with others in order to share information. Networking can take place in many forms, and is helpful for both your current job performance and future advancement. Networking helps to get your name and reputation into the hearts and minds of those who may be in a position to help you advance when you are ready to step up to the next rung on your career ladder. Here are a few ways in which you should network:

- *Professional associations.* Find and join at least one professional association related to your field. These organizations can be local, regional, national, or even international. Attending meetings and conferences will help you learn about current research and/or practices in your field, thus keeping your knowledge base up to date. You will also meet and interact with other professionals in your field and pave the way for the future. The contacts you make in professional organizations will very likely be the foundation of your future career. Get to know the people who are successful, and spend time with them. Get to know their problems and their strategies for success.
- *Community groups or social service organizations.* Participating in organizations such as Toastmasters or Habitat for Humanity will acquaint you with individuals outside of your professional field, but who share your values and interests. As it can in college, volunteerism after graduation can benefit both you and your community.
- *Your college alumni association.* It is useful to keep in touch and stay active with your alumni association after you graduate. You will be able to maintain connections with classmates and older alumni, and will have the opportunity to give back to your alma mater in a variety of ways. These connections and contributions can be quite valuable to your future career advancement.

How Do I Behave as a Professional?

Your image as a professional in the workplace is vital to your success. Professionalism is demonstrated on many different levels above and beyond the performance of your job duties. How you relate to your colleagues, your supervisor, and outside constituents; how you manage conflict; how you express yourself verbally and in writing; and last but not least, how you dress each and every day all communicate to others your level of professionalism.

First and foremost, treat all those with whom you interact with courtesy, respect, and a smile. This includes everyone from the CEO to the custodian—you should be nice to those you don't "have" to be nice to! We all have bad days when we would prefer to be screaming than smiling. And when you do have continued difficulty at work, be sure to arrange a private meeting with your supervisor to discuss the matter and to work things out. It is expected that you may have conflicts with coworkers from time to time, or feel overwhelmed with too many projects and too little time. That's normal! But professional behavior means keeping your emotions in check, and relieving your stress at the gym. A worker with a reputation for emotional instability, frequent outbursts, or disrespectful behavior toward others is unlikely to be rewarded.

Good communication skills will also enhance your professional image. Speaking clearly and articulately, with proper grammar and a pleasant tone of voice, will be noticed and appreciated. Don't ever curse (out loud, anyway)! Smile when you speak and show some enthusiasm. If your communication style does not reflect your commitment to and excitement about your job, you are seriously limiting your ability to move forward.

Avoiding office gossip is another way to demonstrate professional communication skills. Gossip is a huge time waster at the office. It also helps to promote rumors that can be hurtful or damaging to you and your colleagues. The last thing your supervisor wants to see is you and your coworkers standing around gossiping. So, try not to initiate gossip. If a business conversation evolves into gossip, politely redirect the conversation toward the task at hand. If your efforts are unsuccessful, invite your colleagues to discuss the matter over lunch or after hours.

Be very careful with written communication as well. The proliferation of e-mail has, in large part, replaced the formal typewritten memo. And many of our e-conversations with friends and family are quite informal. Keep in mind that business e-mail is still formal business communication, and should be composed appropriately. Use proper grammar, spelling, and punctuation. Include the reason for the communication and expectations for a response. Be concise. Later, when you become a recognized professional and highly regarded in your career, you may be able to relax these rules. For now, project yourself as someone who is dependable, professional, and respectful.

Here's an example. Let's say your boss is considering ways to decrease utility costs in the building, and is considering moving to a four-day workweek. He wants you to find out how the others in the building feel about it. You could write,

"Hey everybody,

The boss wants to find out if we want to work 7 am to 6 pm Mon–Thurs to save $$$. Need an answer by next week. Please respond ASAP. Thanks!

D."

A more professional and effective approach would be,

"Colleagues,

Mr. Roberts has asked me to solicit your feedback regarding a possible new work schedule. In the interest of saving money on utilities, Mr. Roberts proposes a 7:00 a.m. to 6:00 p.m. Monday–Thursday work week beginning April 15th. Please respond with your support or concerns by 8:30 a.m. Wednesday, March 25th. I will then pass your responses along to Mr. Roberts for his consideration.

Thank you,

David Jones"

Not only does the more formal memo reflect on David's level of professionalism, it is also more complete, detailed, respectful of his colleagues, and because his instructions are specific, David will be more likely to receive the desired responses in a timely manner and be able to offer his boss a complete and timely report. As mentioned in an earlier chapter, use e-mail only when time allows—do not expect a response in less than a day or two. When time is of the essence, a phone call or personal visit is more appropriate.

One final word about e-mail: do not send anything you do not want your boss or anyone else to read. E-mail messages are not confidential, and can be retrieved by computer professionals even if you have deleted them from your mailbox. Business e-mail conducted on a company computer is also considered the property of the employer. Before you click on "send," double check to be sure all e-mail correspondence is professional, polite, and job-related. E-mail sent in a fit of anger can be forwarded to your boss and will probably come back to haunt you. Don't gamble your future on an emotion that may pass with just a little time and thought.

Finally, consider your wardrobe. Your clothes speak volumes about you. If your clothes are tasteful and professional, fit properly, and are clean, pressed, and in good repair, you send the nonverbal message that you are serious about your job, you are mature, have good judgment, are self-confident, and respect those around you. However, there will be variation in expectations about dress. Your workplace may be very formal and conservative, or it may be quite casual. There may or may not be a written dress code. If your job interview takes place at the company, try to observe what employees at your level are wearing for an indication of general expectations. If your interview is on campus, and you are not sure of the dress code, interview attire will be appropriate for the first day on the job.

Dressing for Success

In *Dressing for the Job*, Sabath (2006) shares a few tips to keep you looking your best and feeling self-confident!

- What does "business casual" mean? In general, business casual for men means trousers, a short-sleeved shirt or golf shirt, and a sport jacket or sweater. For women, business casual usually means a skirt or slacks with a blouse or sweater.
- Schedule regular haircuts. Don't wait until your hair looks like it needs to be cut, and invest in a quality barber or stylist.
- For men: wear an undershirt under your dress shirt. Why? It will protect the shirt from perspiration, and it helps a white shirt look whiter.
- For women: skirt suit or slack suit? Observe the top-level women in your organization. If you do not see them wearing slacks, stick to a skirt suit.
- For men and women: keep a few "emergency back-up" clothing items at the office. A clean and pressed white shirt or blouse, a tie (for men), and a fresh pair of hose (for women) will come in handy for those occasional lunchtime mishaps or other unforeseen clothing snafus.

What If My Coworkers Drive Me Crazy?

A typical full-time job requires your presence for 40 or more hours each week, so you will most likely find yourself spending more time at the office than anywhere else! This stark reality is just one more reason why an effective career planning and job search process is so critical to your future happiness and success. This also underscores the importance of cultivating and maintaining productive, professional, and rewarding relationships with your colleagues. Your colleagues in many ways will become a second family!

By now you've probably had many workgroup experiences similar to those you'll encounter at the office. If you have participated in study groups, or group projects for a class, a sports team, or a campus organization, then you already know the challenges and rewards of teamwork. You also know your own style and preferences for interacting with the members of your group. Do you tend to take a leadership role, or do you prefer to take direction from others? Do you accept feedback or criticism well? Do you participate fully and keep your commitments to the group? How do you deal with conflict?

As with your family members and friends, your relationships with your coworkers are bound to have ups and downs, and interpersonal conflict from time to time is to be expected. Conflict is not necessarily to be avoided, and when dealt with appropriately it can often help groups to resolve issues and move forward. While employers expect college graduates to be effective team players, colleges and universities do not always offer the types of experiences that students need to develop good teamwork skills (Page and Donelan, 2003). It will be wise for you to take advantage of as many team-building opportunities as you can while in college, as learning to manage conflict will be an important career survival skill. The key is not to avoid conflict, but to react and respond appropriately and productively when conflict occurs. While the following tips are somewhat common sense, they are included as a reminder that preservation of productive working relationships should be a priority for you. When conflict occurs,

- *Keep your cool.* As mentioned earlier, angry outbursts or e-mails will not reflect well on your level of professionalism and maturity. Try to take a break and cool off before planning your response to the situation.
- *Pick your battles.* Ask yourself if the resolution of this particular issue is critical to the mission of your work group. Is the source of the conflict related to your job duties, or is it more of a personality issue? If the latter, let it go.
- *Stay on task.* Arguing or complaining will usually not help complete the project or discussion at hand. Keep your group focused on the goal and move forward.
- *Talk to your supervisor.* If interpersonal conflict cannot be resolved, and job tasks are delayed, have a private meeting to ask for guidance on how to proceed. Chances are, your supervisor will have had some experience with the person or the issue at hand.

Can I Date a Coworker?

With all of that time spent working together, you will undoubtedly get to know your colleagues well, and it will be great if you get along with them. You may get along so well that a relationship with one person begins to evolve above and beyond your status as coworkers. It is no secret that many romantic relationships begin in the workplace. While matters of the heart can be unpredictable, there are a few very important issues to consider, should Cupid send an arrow your way.

The first issue concerns the relative rank of each party in the corporate hierarchy. Romantic relationships with supervisors and supervisees are to be avoided at all costs. These are no-win situations. If and when the relationship goes sour, the situation becomes awkward at best. If one party feels jilted and hurt, the situation becomes downright painful. It then becomes difficult to discern if supervisory feedback or reprimands are appropriate or merely spiteful. If the relationship flourishes, on the other hand, perceptions and rumors of preferential treatment for the supervisee by the supervisor will flourish as well. If you feel you cannot live without dating your supervisor or supervisee, consider looking for a job in another organization.

If you and a coworker of the same rank develop a mutual romantic interest, the situation is a little less messy but nonetheless delicate. Proceed slowly and carefully before making the decision to begin dating one another. Your professional reputations—and possibly your jobs—are at stake. The most important

ON-TARGET TIPS

Gender-Based Strategies for Self-Improvement

Women:

- Don't use male standards to judge your competence.

- Retain strengths in building relationships and staying in touch with emotions. Be proud of them.

- Improve your self-motivation. Be more self-assertive. Focus on knowing your own needs and meeting them. Go beyond the idea that this is selfish. It is self-assertive.

- Don't put up with sexual harassment. Know what qualifies as sexual harassment. Report it when it happens.

Men:

- Retain your strengths. Be self-motivated and achievement-oriented.

- Do a better job of understanding your emotions and self. Explore yourself. Ask yourself what kind of person you want to be. Think more about how you want others to perceive you.

- Work on your relationship skills. Give more consideration to the feelings of others. Make relationships a higher priority in your life.

- If you're aggressive and hostile, tone down your anger. Be self-assertive but not overly aggressive. That is, control yourself and your emotions. Work toward better understanding of your own emotions and the feelings of other people.

thing to remember is to keep the romance out of the office. Do not send personal e-mails, talk on the phone about personal matters, touch each other, or be seen together any more than you would were you not dating. It will be critical to demonstrate to your colleagues and your supervisor that the relationship is not detrimental to your job performance. Rightly or wrongly, rumors may run rampant.

What if a coworker feels attracted to you, but you do not feel the same way? If you have explained your feelings to your suitor, but he or she will not leave you alone, the situation can become a legal matter. Sexual harassment is a very serious offense and is prohibited by the federal Civil Rights Act of 1964. Sexual harassment takes many forms, but is generally defined as unwelcome verbal or physical sexual advances that interfere with your work or create a hostile or offensive work environment. Sexual harassment can occur between males and females, or between members of the same sex. It is particularly serious when rejection of or submission to a sexual encounter is the basis for special treatment or opportunity in the workplace. Examples include repeated requests for a date despite consistent refusals; sexually offensive jokes or remarks in your presence; or unwelcome patting or touching. If you feel you are a victim of sexual harassment, report the incident immediately.

What If I Feel Very Different from My Colleagues?

If you are a member of a minority group, you may feel some concern about dealing with stereotypes or discrimination in the workplace. If you are not a member of a minority group, it will be critical for you to seriously consider any personal biases or values that may impact your relationships with your colleagues. Diversity brings new perspectives, ideas, and values that enhance and empower your organization. However, diversity can also bring values and ideas into conflict.

Corporate culture in the U.S. generally values competition, independence, and autonomy. However, based in part on a long history that includes discrimination, disenfranchisement, and poverty, many members of minority cultures have grown up valuing interdependence, family, and sharing (Helfand, 1995). These types of value differences may never be directly addressed, but can greatly impact the way that individuals approach projects, perceive their role within the organization, and communicate with one another. Minorities may feel an uncomfortable disconnect between observed attitudes and behaviors at work, and the values that they maintain at home. Awareness of these differences can go a long way toward facilitating a productive work environment, and open discussion among colleagues is useful as well. Some employers use caucus groups to raise issues and propose solutions to management (Helfand, 1995).

You should understand your rights as an employee so that you can recognize behaviors that violate the law. Discrimination in hiring, promotion, or compensation based on race, color, creed, gender, pregnancy, or national origin is prohibited by the Civil Rights Act of 1964. However, if you've been passed over for a raise or a promotion and you happen to be a member of a minority group, this does not necessarily mean discrimination has occurred. It will be imperative that you determine the rationale for the action before reporting a violation. You will need to take your time and use good judgment as you decide how to proceed.

As the average age of our population continues to increase, the current workplace is also becoming more diverse in terms of age of employees. You may begin your first job after college in your early twenties, only to find yourself working alongside individuals of your parents' or grandparents' age. As mentioned in the previous chapter, older employees serve the organization well in many ways: they tend to be very productive and very patient, have a strong work ethic and a good attitude, and generally stay with an employer for a long time. Younger colleagues have much to learn from their senior coworkers.

If, on the other hand, you are quite a bit older than most of your peers at the office, you may feel a little anxious or intimidated about competing for promotions or raises. If this becomes the case, Helfand (1995) suggests some strategies to help you feel more competent and competitive:

- *Exercise!* Older adults who stay healthy and physically fit will have more energy and self-confidence and will miss work less often.
- *Continually update your computer skills.* Our current generation of traditional-age college graduates will often have the edge on new technology.
- *Emphasize your past professional experiences*, but avoid too many references that emphasize your age (i.e., "back in the day," or "when I was your age").
- *Update your wardrobe.* If your business attire from 25 years ago still fits, congratulations! Now go shopping and treat yourself to a few new outfits that are tasteful and current, but not too trendy.

As with race and color, discrimination based on age is also illegal. The Age Discrimination in Employment Act of 1967 prohibits employers from passing over employees for promotions or raises based on age. The earlier discussion of risks and benefits regarding charges of racial discrimination apply here as well. Do your homework to determine if indeed discrimination has occurred before filing a complaint.

A final type of diversity that you may encounter at work involves people with disabilities, or the "differently abled." A wheelchair user is an example of a person with a very visible disability, but there are invisible disabilities as well: people with AIDS or mental disorders, or those who are recovering alcoholics are coping with very serious issues of which colleagues may or may not be aware.

If you have a disability, the most important quality you can communicate to your employer is a positive attitude. Express your enthusiasm and optimism, and focus on your strengths, not your limitations. If your disability is not visible, and will not impact your job performance, it is up to you whether or not you wish to disclose your condition to your employer. If you work with colleagues who have disabilities, keep the following statistic in mind: five out of every six people with disabilities were not born with the disabilities, but acquired them later in life (Helfand, 1995). This statistic reminds us to be especially sensitive to the trauma that the differently abled may have experienced and may still be learning to cope with.

If you have a disability and it does impact your ability to perform your job, you do have legal protection. The Americans with Disabilities Act of 1990 prohibits employers from discrimination against disabled people in hiring, promotion, or compensation and requires them to provide reasonable accommodations, such as modification of the job duties, equipment, or work schedule when possible. If no type of accommodation would enable you to perform the essential functions of a job, however, employers are not legally required to hire or promote you. If discrimination occurs, and you wish to file a complaint, contact the Equal Employment Opportunity office.

Attitude Is Everything

Employers will appreciate and reward an employee who demonstrates consistent optimism, cheerfulness, enthusiasm, and a "can-do" attitude even when circumstances are gloomy. As a newbie in the workforce, or a career changer, you may be facing a steep learning curve in your new position, and you may make a mistake or two along the way. Making excuses, blaming others, or beating up on yourself will only hurt you. Have you ever been around someone who complains constantly and wallows in negativity? Did you feel uncomfortable? Did it drag you down? Perpetual pessimism will get you nowhere in your relationships with your boss and your colleagues. Decide now to take responsibility for your actions, understand mistakes are part of life, and commit yourself to an "attitude of gratitude," each and every day.

On Your Campus

Plan to attend the next university commencement ceremony on your campus. Take in the sights, sounds, and excitement. Imagine yourself in cap and gown, on your graduation day, surrounded by family, faculty, and friends. (See Appendix G for an explanation of academic dress.)

Visualize your commencement day and think of it often. Don't lose sight of your goals!

Can I Be My Own Boss?

In order to remain competitive, large employers are expected to continue downsizing in the near future. New technologies, including electronic commerce, allow companies to function more efficiently, while eliminating some of the most costly of resources: personnel (Krannich, 2002). The traditional path of long-term employment with a Fortune 500 company may be more the exception than the rule in the coming decades. So if you have ever dreamed of owning your own business, now may be the time.

Many college students dream of being their own boss. They may desire to avoid a long commute, have flexible hours, or spend more time at home with children. They may be inventive, creative, have fresh ideas, and be willing to take the risks associated with becoming an entrepreneur. If you think this might be for you, either immediately after graduation or even down the road a little way, there are some important considerations to keep in mind.

First, recognize the risks. About half of all new businesses fail within the first three years, and about 90 percent fail within ten years (Krannich, 2002). These sobering statistics underscore the need for careful planning and research before venturing out on your own. There are no guarantees that any new business will survive. But success can be the reward of a lifetime. So if you're still game, read on!

While you're in college, consider expanding the breadth of your curriculum. For example, working for yourself means that you will have to know a lot about a great many different areas, including accounting, legal matters affecting hiring and personnel practices, advertising, marketing, and others. You may have to be an expert in all of these areas. Consider course work in accounting, marketing, management, psychology, sociology, and also courses related to your intended industry. An interdisciplinary degree may be of interest.

In *What Color Is Your Parachute*, Bolles (2005) describes a step-by-step process that you can adopt to identify the specific knowledge and skills for a particular self-employment goal. Dubbed "A – B = C," here's how it works:

- First, visit with three individuals who are at least 50 to 75 miles away from you who own a business similar to the one you want to start. Why so far away? Businesses in your local community will be competing with you for business. Ask these individuals what skills and resources are necessary for their success, what obstacles or problems they've encountered, and what advice they now have for someone starting out. This information will become your list "A."
- Then, make a list of all of your own skills, relevant knowledge, and resources that you currently have to devote to your business. This list becomes list "B."
- Finally, subtract the items on list "B" from list "A" to create a list of the skills and knowledge that you need to acquire. This becomes your list "C." You can use this information to begin to tailor your college experience toward your self-employment goals.

What industries are promising for new businesses? Krannich (2002) identifies several social trends and corresponding opportunities. Because our population is becoming older, services for the elderly, such as health care, housing, transportation, mortuaries, and cemeteries will grow in demand over the coming years. A second area of demand targets busy families—any type of Internet-based shopping or service that helps eliminate time spent driving or waiting in line will also grow in demand.

There are many resources available to help you consider if entrepreneurship is for you, and it is beyond the scope of this book to give you all the information you are likely to need, but consider starting with the Small Business Administration (http://www.sba.gov/) or SCORE (http://www.score.org/). Each of these organizations can provide valuable information, without charge, to help you make the dream of owning your own business a reality.

? Questions for Class Discussion

1. How does campus culture differ from corporate culture?
2. Is it okay to date your boss as long as the two of you keep it a secret?
3. Should conflict at work be avoided? Why or why not?
4. How does it make you feel to consider that there is "no syllabus at work"?
5. Is diversity an issue on your campus? Why or why not?
6. How many of you would prefer to be self-employed? In what industries?

Activity

What is your goal after graduation? Will you be working for a large corporation? Will you begin graduate school? Or will you start your own business? Whatever your goal, this activity can help you learn more about the realities of your intended career path.

1. Identify two professional associations related to your intended field. For each, include the full name, Web site or contact information, and membership requirements.

2. On your campus or in your community, identify one individual who is working in a position you think you would enjoy. If you are considering graduate school, this could be a graduate student. Arrange for a 20-minute interview. Consider the following questions:
    a. What do you love most about what you do? What do like the least?
    b. What types of experiences do you think best prepared you for your current position?
    c. If you were to repeat your undergraduate college experience, what would you do differently?
    d. What was your greatest challenge during your first year on the job (or in the graduate program)?

3. After the interview, write a one- to two-page summary of the discussion. Then answer this question: Are you still interested in this particular job? Why or why not?

Journal Assignment

What will your world be like during your next life transition? Reflect on your current daily challenges and the new challenges that you will face as you begin your career or graduate school. Write one to two pages. To direct your writing, please consider these questions:

1. Describe your professional goals or plans for advanced study.
2. What expectations do you have about entering the world of work or graduate school?
3. What will be the greatest challenges for you during the first year after graduation?
4. What strategies will you adopt to successfully overcome these challenges?

Summary

- The transition from college to work will be a major life change, similar to the transition from one college to another.

- Unlike the typical college classroom, expectations in the workplace may be ill-defined or poorly communicated.
- A mentor can help you to adapt to the new environment and help you to thrive and succeed.
- Professional dress, communication, and behavior are critical to career success and advancement.
- Professional relationships and good teamwork skills are expected in the workplace.
- Diversity in race, age, and ability must be acknowledged and embraced.
- Self-employment can be risky but also extremely rewarding for some graduates.

Case Study

Ron loved computers. In high school, he tended to spend a lot of time using and learning about new technology. As a rather introverted young man, he did not enjoy the company of other people and spent a lot of time alone. But that suited Ron just fine. Upon graduation from high school, Ron was not sure of his interest in a four-year college degree, so he decided to pursue an associate's degree in computer science with the goal of becoming a programmer. Upon graduation, he worked for several years for a large online retailer, programming and updating Web pages. This position suited him quite well, as he was able to work from home most of the time. When he did report to the office, Ron did not interact very much with others, and could come and go as he wished. He always wore casual, comfortable clothes, such as jeans or sweats, and tied his long hair back in a ponytail.

After several years Ron felt ready to advance his career. He decided to complete his bachelor's degree in computer science, so that he would be competitive for an administrative position. All of his plans fell into place, and upon graduation Ron landed a job as a computer network administrator at a local bank. He was in charge of two supervisees and enjoyed a substantial salary increase from his previous job.

Ron's personal habits and preferences were well entrenched by this point, and he really had no intention of changing his working style or his wardrobe despite the much more conservative atmosphere at the bank. After all, Ron reasoned, he did not interact directly with customers, got along with his supervisees, and kept the computer networks functioning perfectly. Ron's supervisor encouraged him to dress more professionally, but Ron felt insulted by this—clearly his job performance had nothing to do with his style of dress. He owned one suit and tie, which he wore only to the job interview, and he had no intention of donning a coat and tie from now on.

Ron also refused to participate in company social events, such as birthday parties or Friday afternoon softball games. His colleagues soon gave up on asking him to come out of his cubicle, as the grouchy response was always the same: "I've got work to do!"

Ron so despised being around other people that he frequently worked late into the evening, after everyone else had gone home. After a late evening at the office he would frequently oversleep and come in at 9:30 or 10 a.m. the next day. He ignored his supervisor's warnings about tardiness, assuming it did not matter because the computer networks were functioning well and any problems that occurred were always quickly resolved.

About two years later, Ron's supervisor retired, and Ron applied for his position. He assumed he would be a shoe-in for the job based on his excellent technical skills, knowledge of the company computer systems, and the respect that he had earned from his supervisees. When an outside applicant with the same amount of experience was hired, Ron was mystified.

Food for Thought

What mistakes did Ron make during his first year on the job? What could he have done to better adapt to his new corporate culture? Why do you believe he was passed over for the promotion?

Appendix A

My Long-Term Academic Plan – Sample

Date: *August 2008*

Hours Complete to Date: *62*

Hours Remaining: *60*

My Major Is: *Psychology*

My Minor Is: *Spanish*

Other requirements (i.e. Pre-Health, Teacher Certification, Second Major or Minor, etc.)

Pre-Med

Anticipated Graduation Date: *Spring 2010*

Term: Fall 2008, 15 hours	Term: Spring 2009, 14 hours	Term: Summer 2009
**Organic Chemistry I	**Organic Chemistry II	
	**Organic Chemistry Lab	
**Statistics	**Research Methods I	Elective?
**Intermediate Spanish I	**Intermediate Spanish II	(if decide to go to summer School then need just 13
*Humanities	*Speech Communication	Hours next fall!)
*American History		

Term: Fall 2009, 16 hours	Term: Spring 2010, 15 hours	Term: Summer 2010
**Research Methods II	**Senior Seminar	
*Spanish Literature I	**Spanish Literature II	
*Personality Theories	*Physiological Psychology	
**Clinical Psychology	*Elective	
*Elective		

* Indicates course requirement that is flexible — could take in alternate semester or summer

** Indicates course requirement that is sequential or offered only in specified semesters — must take in order indicated

Notes

1. Take MCAT April 2009!
2. Clinical Psych only offered every other fall semester!

Appendix B
Sample Outline of a Research Paper

STUDENT TEAMS AS THERAPY GROUPS

How progress and conflict follow strikingly similar patterns.

AUTHOR, CLASS OR ASSIGNMENT, DATE

ABSTRACT

This study attempts to draw comparisons between college students working closely in a team environment with patterns of interaction in psychotherapy groups. The literature indicates similarities ... (More)

INTRODUCTION

Much has been written about the formation, organization and effectiveness of student work teams (Bacon, Stewart, Silver, 1999; Page and Donelan, 2003; Caspersz, Wu, Skene, 2003). The practice of grouping students ... (More)

LITERATURE

Student Teams

Faculty and advisers responsible for oversight of student work groups have long observed that successful teams go through a fairly predictable pattern of development (Bacon, Stewart, Silver, 1999; Goodwin, Campbell and Wolter, 1997). (More)

Psychotherapy Groups

The texts and research dealing with group counseling in psychotherapy have drawn some interesting conclusions about the patterns of progress that become evident as the groups evolve. (More)

HYPOTHESES

After careful review of the literature on both student teams and therapy groups, it is expected that there will be similarities between the processes through each operate to achieve their objectives. (More)

METHODOLOGY

This study sought to explore similarities between a student work team and the experience of psychotherapy groups as both groups work toward a common goal. In the case of the students, the goal is to work together to accomplish a task and benefit individually. (More)

RESULTS

It is important to note here that analyses of this type are not intended to demonstrate much in the way of statistical evidence, but to rely on clear patterns and shifts . . . (More)

DISCUSSION

The purpose of this study was to examine the similarities between working groups in two very different situations. It has long been observed that there are particular problems and challenges . . . (More)

BIBLIOGRAPHY

Bacon, D. R., Stewart, K. A. and Silver, W. S., 1999, "Lessons From the Best and worst Student Team Experiences: How a Teacher Can Make A Difference," *Journal of Management Education*, Oct. v. 23, n. 5.

Barker, R. T., Franzak, F. J., 1997, "Team Building in the Classroom: Preparing Students for their Organizational Future," *Journal of Technical Writing and Communication*, v. 27, n. 3.

(More)

Appendix C

My Number One Goal:

Priority Activity related to that goal:

Secondary Goal:

Priority Activity related to that goal:

How Do I Spend My Time?

	MON	TUES	WED	THURS	FRI	SAT	SUN
5 AM							
5:30							
6 AM							
6:30							
7 AM							
7:30							
8 AM							
8:30							
9 AM							
9:30							
10 AM							
10:30							
11 AM							
11:30							
12 PM							
12:30							
1 PM							
1:30							
2 PM							
2:30							
3 PM							
3:30							
4 PM							
4:30							
5 PM							
5:30							
6 PM							
6:30							
7 PM							
7:30							
8 PM							
8:30							

	MON	TUES	WED	THURS	FRI	SAT	SUN
9 PM							
9:30							
10 PM							
10:30							
11 PM							
11:30							
12 AM							
12:30							
1 AM							
1:30							
2 AM							
2:30							
3 AM							
3:30							
4 AM							
4:30							

My Ideal Weekly Calendar

	MON	TUES	WED	THURS	FRI	SAT	SUN
5 AM							
5:30							
6 AM							
6:30							
7 AM							
7:30							
8 AM							
8:30							
9 AM							
9:30							
10 AM							
10:30							
11 AM							
11:30							
12 PM							
12:30							
1 PM							
1:30							
2 PM							
2:30							
3 PM							
3:30							

	MON	TUES	WED	THURS	FRI	SAT	SUN
4 PM							
4:30							
5 PM							
5:30							
6 PM							
6:30							
7 PM							
7:30							
8 PM							
8:30							
9 PM							
9:30							
10 PM							
10:30							
11 PM							
11:30							
12 AM							
12:30							
1 AM							
1:30							
2 AM							
2:30							
3 AM							
3:30							
4 AM							
4:30							

Appendix D
Monthly Personal Finance Worksheet

1. *Fixed Expenses*
    Rent, mortgage, or residence hall $_____
    Car payment $_____
    Car insurance $_____
    Tuition and fees $_____
    _____ $_____
    _____ $_____

2. *Variable Expenses*
    Groceries $_____
    Telephone $_____
    Cable $_____
    Internet $_____
    Electric $_____
    Entertainment (dining out, CD's, hobbies) $_____
    Personal care (shampoo, laundry supplies, etc.) $_____
    Medical care (medicine, doctor visits) $_____
    _____ $_____
    _____ $_____
    _____ $_____
    _____ $_____

    Total Monthly Expenses $_____

3. *Income*
    Employment $_____
    Scholarships and Grants $_____
    Loans $_____
    _____ $_____
    _____ $_____

    Total Monthly Income $_____
    Difference $_____

Appendix E

Sample Career Planning Guide

In order to be competitive in the job market after you graduate, you will need to take advantage of every opportunity to build your resume and refine your skills while you are still in college. Traditional four-year planning guides may not fit you as a transfer or nontraditional student, so the following guide groups tasks chronologically into three phases – once you've completed the tasks in Phase One, move on to Phase Two, and finally Phase Three (this should be your final year in college).

Phase One

Visit your campus Career Services office. Become familiar with the services and resources available, such as resume assistance, mock interviews, assessment tools, reference books, or personal counseling.

Identify your primary career goal. Find out how much education, training, or special skills will be required for entry into this field. Research job locations, starting salaries, and rate of growth for this profession.

Join at least one student, community, or professional organization related to your career goal that will enable you to earn leadership experience, learn more about your chosen profession, and network with current professionals in your field.

Schedule a meeting with at least one professor who teaches a course related to your chosen career, and discuss your interests and goals. Ask this professor for guidance regarding campus or other opportunities that will help prepare you for entry into your field.

Identify part-time jobs, internships, or volunteer experience available during the school year or during the summer related to your career goal. Find out how to apply, and plan to complete at least one such experience prior to graduation.

Phase Two

Write your resume. Seek assistance and feedback from your Career Services office. Identify any gaps in experience or skills that need to be filled prior to graduation. Update your resume on a regular basis.

Attend career fairs on campus. Practice introducing yourself to prospective employers, and gather information about hiring trends in your chosen field. Research employers of interest.

Attend at least one professional meeting or conference of an association related to your career goal. Introduce yourself to members of the association and let them know of your interests and goals.

If you're considering graduate school, research prospective schools and obtain application information including deadlines, required exam scores (such as the GRE or LSAT), letters of recommendation, and other application materials.

Arrange for at least one mock interview with your career services office.

Phase Three

Begin your job search. Utilize contacts you have made via professional or community organizations, your professors, internship or volunteer supervisors, career services job postings, specific company employment listings, and the internet to compile a list of upcoming opportunities.

Identify and register for on-campus services such as employer interviews or online resume posting provided by your career services office.

Obtain the proper interview attire. A leather portfolio or case is a good idea as well.

If you are applying to graduate school, be sure to take the required admissions test in time for scores to be delivered in advance of the application deadline.

Keep detailed records of all cover letters and resumes sent. Follow up with a phone call as necessary. Send a thank-you letter after each interview.

After you have obtained your first job, be sure to thank all those who helped you along the way. Keep in touch with your school – you may be in a position to help future generations with their career goals!

Appendix F

Sample Chronological Resume

Carmen Gonzales
123 University Avenue, Apt. 10
College Town, CA 98765
123.456.7890 (cell)
Carmen@college.edu

Objective: To assist alcohol or drug dependent clients in the process of recovery as a Drug and Alcohol Counselor

Education

- Bachelor of Arts, Sociology. State University, May, 2008. GPA 3.78
  - Minor, Women's Studies
- County Community College, 30 hours of general studies completed, 1982–1984

Experience

- *Student Assistant, State University Office of Financial Aid,* January 2006–present (half-time work study position). Greet students as they enter office, assess needs; answer telephones, direct calls; schedule appointments with financial counselors; maintain literature racks and keep waiting area clean and organized.
- *Home Health Care Aide, Health Care Associates, Greenville,* CA, July 1995–July 2005 (half-time position). Visited elderly clients in their homes; assisted with meal preparation, bathing and grooming, laundry and routine household tasks; monitored physical symptoms.
- *Hostess; Pete's Pizza & Pasta, Greenville,* CA, June 1981–January 1985. Greeted customers; assigned seating; answered telephone; made reservations; processed take-out orders.

Activities

- President, State University Sociology Club, August 2007–present
- Vice-President, State University Sociology Club, August 2006–June 2007
- Volunteer, College Town Big Brothers/Big Sisters, August 2005–present

Honors and Awards

- Department of Sociology Outstanding Senior Award, 2007–2008
- Dean's List, Fall 2005, Spring 2006, Fall 2006, Spring 2007

Special Skills

- Proficient in Mac and PC; Microsoft Office; SPSS
- Fluent in Spanish

References available upon request

Sample Functional Resume

Carmen Gonzales
123 University Avenue, Apt. 10
College Town, CA 98765
123.456.7890 (cell)
Carmen@college.edu

Objective: To assist alcohol or drug dependent clients in the process of recovery as a Drug and Alcohol Counselor

Summary of Qualifications

- Over 15 years experience in service roles, assessing individual needs, providing assistance or referring to appropriate resources.
- Demonstrated leadership, teamwork, and managerial skills.
- Fluent in Spanish language and familiar with Hispanic culture.
- Proficient with computer software and hardware, including Microsoft Office and SPSS.

Accomplishments

- *Initiated State University Alcohol Use Assessment and Intervention Program, 2007 fall term.* With support from the Office of Student Affairs, surveyed over 2500 SU students regarding use or abuse of alcohol. Results were used to design a campus-wide alcohol awareness and intervention program.
    - o Program resulted in a 25% overall decrease in self-reported student alcohol use (spring 2008 follow-up data).
- *Revised and improved intake procedure for walk-in traffic at the State University Office of Financial Aid.* Created computer kiosks in the lobby area to track student questions and concerns regarding financial aid. Program linked questions to the student's electronic file and alerted the appropriate financial counselor via instant messenger.
    - o Reduced average wait time from a minimum of 20 minutes to less than six.

Experience

- *Student Assistant, State University Office of Financial Aid,* January 2006–present
- *Home Health Care Aide, Health Care Associates,* Greenville, CA, July 1995–July 2005
- *Hostess, Pete's Pizza & Pasta,* Greenville, CA, June 1981–January 1985.
- *Volunteer, College Town Big Brothers/Big Sisters,* August 2005–present
- *President, State University Sociology Club,* August 2007–present

Education

- Bachelor of Arts, Sociology. State University, May, 2008. GPA 3.78
    - o Minor, Women's Studies
- County Community College, 30 hours of general studies completed, 1982–1984

References available upon request

Sample Combination Resume

Carmen Gonzales
123 University Avenue, Apt. 10
College Town, CA 98765
123.456.7890 (cell)
Carmen@college.edu

Objective: To assist alcohol or drug dependent clients in the process of recovery as a Drug and Alcohol Counselor

Profile

- Helped to significantly decrease use of alcohol on the State University campus
- Restructured and improved efficiency of intake process in SU Financial Aid
- Assisted over 50 elderly clients live independently over a ten-year period
- Mentored three young girls as a Big Sister over a two-year period

Experience

- *Student Assistant, State University Office of Financial Aid,* January 2006–present (half-time work-study position). Greet students as they enter office, determine theirneeds; answer telephones, direct calls; schedule appointments with financial counselors; maintain literature racks and keep waiting area clean and organized.
  - o Reduced wait time for walk-in traffic via a computerized intake system.
- *Home Health Care Aide, Health Care Associates,* July 1995–July 2005 (half-time position). Visited elderly clients in their homes; assisted with meal preparation; bathing and grooming; laundry and routine household tasks; monitored physical symptoms.
  - o Assisted over 50 clients remain active and independent.

Honors and Awards

- State University Department of Sociology Outstanding Senior Award, 2007–2008
- State University Dean's List, Fall 2005, Spring 2006, Fall 2006, Spring 2007

Special Skills

- Proficient in Mac and PC; Microsoft Office; SPSS
- Fluent in Spanish

Education

- Bachelor of Arts, Sociology. State University, May, 2008. GPA 3.78
  - o Minor, Women's Studies
- County Community College, 30 hours of general studies completed, 1982–1984

References available upon request

Sample Cover Letter

123 University Avenue, Apt. 10
College Town, CA 98765

May 1, 2008

Ms. Deborah Smith
Director
Recovery Counseling Services Center
800 River Drive
Anytown, CA 98765

Dear Ms. Smith:

I respectfully submit this application for the position of Drug and Alcohol Counselor, as advertised on the State University Career Center web site. I believe my education, experience, and special skills will be a perfect match for the position.

My life experiences have been devoted to helping others in need, as my resume will attest. The educational background that I have earned at State University has provided me with a solid foundation in the theory and practice of social services. My specific interest in and preparation for working with alcohol and drug dependent clients evolved during my tenure as a volunteer with College Town Big Brothers/Big Sisters. This experience dramatically raised my awareness of the tragic impact that substance abuse has on children and families. As a volunteer, I successfully mentored several young girls and helped connect them and their families with the appropriate community resources and other assistance programs.

Last fall, as President of the State University Sociology Club, I initiated a drug and alcohol awareness program to help State University students assess and curb their levels of alcohol use. The program was quite successful, and in part prompted the Sociology Department to name me as the 2006-2007 Outstanding Senior.

My overall level of maturity, life experiences, and educational background will help me earn your clients' trust and respect. In addition, my fluency in the Spanish language will be an asset with your growing Hispanic clientele. I look forward to discussing the position with you in more detail soon. I can be reached at 123.456.7890 anytime. Thank you very much for your consideration of this application.

Sincerely,

Carmen Gonzales

Carmen Gonzales

Appendix G

Caps, Gowns, and Hoods—A Brief History

Academic regalia is the term used to describe the caps, gowns, and hoods worn during commencement ceremonies and other formal academic events. If you've been to a university commencement in the past, you probably observed a wide variety of regalia worn by faculty and graduating students. Have you ever wondered about the meaning behind all of the colors and shapes?

Rules governing academic regalia date back to Europe in the 12th and 13th centuries. Due to connections with the church, students and faculty wore robes similar to those worn by clergy. Rather than serving a ceremonial purpose as they do today, long gowns and hoods in medieval times were also useful for warmth and were worn every day.

As universities began to develop in the United States, these clothing traditions were extended, although Americans did not choose to wear regalia daily. Rather, it was reserved for formal occasions. The style and color of regalia was based on European tradition, but it did not yet have any formal guidelines.

In 1932, the American Council on Education created a code for the styles, colors, and shapes of caps, gowns, and hoods; this code is still used today. Because the code is not a law, deviation is possible, but most universities choose to follow these guidelines.

Gowns: Gowns are usually long and black with differences in the shapes of the sleeves. Bachelor sleeves are pointed, master sleeves are oblong, and doctoral sleeves are bell-shaped. In addition, a doctoral gown has velvet trim on the front of the gown and on the sleeves that often signifies the academic discipline of the degree holder via a specific color. The fabric is generally cotton, wool, rayon, or silk.

Caps: Caps may be of a fabric to match the gown, but only doctors may wear a velvet cap. A tassel is worn with the cap and may be black or the color of the wearer's academic discipline. Doctoral tassels may be gold.

Hoods: A hood is black with a colorful lining that reflects the colors of the institution granting the degree. Bachelors' hoods are three feet long; masters' hoods are three and one-half feet long; and doctoral hoods are four feet long. Although an individual may hold more than one academic degree, only one hood (the highest level earned) may be worn. Many American universities do not supply hoods for bachelor's candidates; rather hoods are used only for master's and doctoral candidates.

Although many students choose not to observe the code regarding what is worn underneath the gown, the American Council on Education recommends wearing clothes and shoes of an appropriate dark color that harmonize with the gown (Sullivan, 2005).

References

Adelman, C. 2006. *The Toolbox Revisited: Paths to Degree Completion from High School Through College.* Washington, D.C.: U.S. Department of Education.

Albion, M. 2000. *Making a Life, Making a Living: Reclaiming Your Purpose and Passion in Business and in Life.* New York: Warner Business Books.

American Consumer Credit Counseling. 2005. Retrieved November 1, 2005 from **http://www.consumercredit.com/docs/CreditWebpdf.pdf**

Andreatta, B. 2006. *Navigating the Research University.* Boston: Thomson Wadsworth.

Bacon D. R., K. A. Stewart, and W. S. Silver. 1999. Lessons from the best and worst student team experiences: how a teacher can make a difference. *Journal of Management Education, 23*(5), 467-488, October.

Bank of America. 2005. Bank of America survey finds New York college students' personal finances don't make the grade. Retrieved February 4, 2006 from **http://www.keepmedia.com/pubs/PRNewswire/2005/10/25/1061080**

Berkner, L., S. He, and E. F. Cataldi. 2002. Descriptive summary of 1995–96 beginning postsecondary students: six years later. National Center for Educational Statistics. Retrieved February 4, 2006 from **http://nces.ed.gov/pubs2003/2003151.pdf**

Bolles, R. N. 2005. *What Color is Your Parachute?* Berkeley, CA: Ten Speed Press.

Bridges, W. 2003. *Managing Transitions: Making the Most of Change.* 2nd ed., Cambridge, MA: Perseus Books Group.

Brown, L. B. 2005. College students can benefit by participating in a prepaid meal plan. *Journal of the American Dietetic Association, 105*(3), 445–448.

Caspersz, D., R. Wu, J. Skene. 2003. Factors influencing effective performance of university student teams. *Proceedings of the HERDSA Conference*, Christchurch, New Zealand, *26.*

Cohen, A. M. 1998. *The Shaping of American Higher Education.* San Francisco: Jossey–Bass.

College Board. 2005. 2005–06 College costs. Retrieved February 4, 2006 from **http://www.collegeboard.com/article/0,3868,6-29-0-4494,00.html**

Core Institute. 2004. *Core Alcohol and Drug Survey.* Carbondale, IL: Southern Illinois University.

Covey, S. 1998. *The Seven Habits of Highly Effective Teens: The Ultimate Teenage Success Guide.* New York: Simon & Schuster.

Davies, T. and E. Dickmann. 1998. Student voices in the transfer process: Do we hear them? Do we listen? *Community College Journal of Research and Practice, 22*(5), 541–557.

Ellis, D. 2006. *Becoming a Master Student.* Boston: Houghton Mifflin.

Engler, B. 1999. *Personality Theories.* 5th ed. Boston: Houghton Mifflin.

Ferguson Publishing Company. 2001. *The Top 100: The Fastest Growing Careers for the 21st Century.* Chicago: Ferguson.

Ferreria, S. E., M. T. de Mello, M. V. Rossi, and M. L. Souza-Formigoni. 2004. Does an energy drink modify the effects of alcohol in a maximal effort test? *Alcoholism: Clinical and Experimental Research, 28*(9), 1408–1412.

Girard, J. 1979. *How to Sell Yourself.* New York: Warner Books, Inc.

Gleitman, H. 1996. *Basic Psychology.* New York: W.W. Norton & Company, Inc.

Goodwin, C., A. Campbell, R. Wolter. 1997. Student work groups/teams: current practices in an engineering and technology curriculum compared to models found in team development literature. *27th Annual Proceedings of the ASEE Frontiers in Education Conference, 1,* 214.

Grites, T. J. 2004. Redefining the role: reflections and directions. In T. J. Kerr, M. C. King, and T. J. Grites (Eds.), Advising transfer students: issues and strategies. *NACADA Journal, 12,* 123-132.

Hallberg, E., K. Hallberg, and R. Aschieris. 2004. *Making the Dean's List.* Belmont, CA: Wadsworth.

Hawk, B. S. 1998. *What Employers Really Want.* Chicago: VGM Career Horizons.

Helfand, D. P. 1995. *Career Change.* Lincolnwood, IL: NTC Publishing Group.

Hingson, R., T. Heeren, M. Winter, and H. Wechsler. 2005. Magnitude of alcohol-related mortality and morbidity among U.S. college students ages 18–24: Changes from 1998–2001. *Annual Review of Public Health, 26,* 259–279.

Holmes, T. 2005. The true cost of a low credit score. Bankrate.com. Retrieved February 6, 2006 from
http://www.bankrate.com/brm/news/debt/debtcreditguide/different-scores1.asp

Hsu, L. K. 1990. *Eating Disorders.* New York: Guilford Press.

King, J. E. 1998. Too many students are working too many hours. *Chronicle of Higher Education,* A72.

Koch, N. and K. W. Wasson. 2002. *The Transfer Student's Guide to the College Experience.* Boston: Houghton Mifflin.

Krannich, R. 2002. *Change Your Job, Change Your Life.* Manassas Park, VA: Impact Publications.

Laanan, F. S. (Ed.). 2001. Transfer students: trends and issues . *New Directions for Community Colleges,* No. 114, Vol. 30, No. 2. San Francisco: Jossey-Bass.

Litt, A. S. 2000. *The College Student's Guide to Eating Well on Campus.* Bethesda, MD: Tulip Hill Press.

Lynch, R. 1994. *Seamless Education: Barriers to Transfer in Postsecondary Education.* (Briefing Paper No. 3). Athens: University of Georgia, Department of Occupational Studies.

National Association of Colleges and Employers. 2006. Organizations Google/review job candidate profiles on social networking sites. Retrieved August 30, 2006 from
http://www.naceweb.org/press/display.asp?year=&prid=240

National Center for Education Statistics. 2004. Descriptive summary of 1995-96 beginning postsecondary students: six years later. Retrieved November 23, 2006, from
http://nces.ed.gov/programs/quarterly/vol_5/5_1/q5_2.asp#H8

National Center for Education Statistics. 2004. Digest of education statistics. Retrieved November 23, 2006, from **http://nces.ed.gov/programs/digest/d04/ch_3.asp**

National Center for Education Statistics. 2005. National postsecondary student aid study. Retrieved February 4, 2006 from **http://nces.ed.gov/surveys/npsas/index.asp**

National Center for Education Statistics. 2006. The condition of education 2006. Retrieved December 10, 2006 from **http://nces.ed.gov/fastfacts/display.asp?id=77**

Nist, S. and J. P. Holschuh. 2002. *College Rules: How to Study, Survive, and Succeed in College.* Berkeley, CA: Ten Speed Press.

Nowak, M. 2004. *Understanding the Community College Transfer Experience from the Student Voice.* Unpublished doctoral dissertation, Boston College.

Page, D. and J. G. Donelan. 2003. Team building skills for students. *Journal of Education for Business, 78* (3).

Peck, P. 2001. WebMD Medical News. Retrieved February 4, 2006 from **http://www.webmd.com/content/article/33/1728_82596.htm#**

Pew Internet andAmerican Life Project. 2004. The mainstreaming of online life. Retrieved February 4, 2006 from **http://www.pewinternet.org/pdfs/Internet_Status_2005.pdf**

Porot, D. 1999. *The 101 Toughest Interview Questions . . . and Answers that Win the Job.* Berkeley, CA: Ten Speed Press.

Sabath, A. M. 2006. Dressing for the job. *Job Choices: Diversity Edition, 49,* 59–60.

Santrock, J. W. and J. S. Halonen. 2004. *Your Guide to College Success: Strategies for Achieving Your Goals.* Belmont, CA: Wadsworth.

Sturgeon, J. 2005. Bad credit hurts in many ways. Retrieved February 4, 2006 from **http://www.bankrate.com/brm/news/debt/debtcreditguide/credit-hurts1.asp**

Sullivan, E. 2005. An academic costume code and an academic ceremony guide. American Council on Education. Retrieved February 4, 2006 from **http://www.acenet.edu**

Tanabe, G. and K. Tanabe. 2004. *501 Ways for Adult Students to Pay for College.* Los Altos, CA: SuperCollege, LLC.

U.S. Census Bureau. 2006. Current Population Survey, 2006 Annual Social and Economic Supplement. Retrieved November 23, 2006 from **http://pubdb3.census.gov/macro/032006/perinc/new03_000.htm**

U.S. Department of Agriculture. 2005. Dietary guidelines for Americans. Retrieved November 13, 2005 from **http://www.health.gov/dietaryguidelines/dga2005/ report/**

Von Oech, R. 1998. *A Whack on the Side of the Head.* New York: Warner Books, Inc.

Wahlstrom, C., B. Williams, and P. Shea. 2003. *The Successful Distance Learning Student.* Belmont, CA: Wadsworth.

Warnick, M. 2005. Credit card minimum payments rising. Bankrate.com. Retrieved February 4, 2006 from **http://www.bankrate.com/brm/news/debt/20050503a2.asp**

Wilkinson, R. 2005. What colleges must do to help needy students. *The Chronicle of Higher Education, 52*(7), B7.